The War on Drugs

The War on Drugs

David L. Hudson Jr.

SERIES EDITOR
Alan Marzilli, M.A., J.D.

CHELSEA HOUSE
An Infobase Learning Company

The War on Drugs

Chelsea House
An imprint of Infobase Learning
132 West 31st Street
New York, NY 10001

Library of Congress Cataloging-in-Publication Data
Hudson, David L., 1969–
The war on drugs / By David L. Hudson Jr.
p. cm. — (Point/Counterpoint.)
Includes bibliographical references and index.
ISBN 978-1-60413-758-3 (hardcover)
1. Drugs—Law and legislation—United States. 2. Drug control—United States. 3. Drug abuse—United States—Prevention. 4. Drug legalization—United States. I. Title.
KF3885.H83 2011
363.450973—dc22   2010052649

Chelsea House books are available at special discounts when purchased in bulk quantities for businesses, associations, institutions, or sales promotions. Please call our Special Sales Department in New York at (212) 967-8800 or (800) 322-8755.

You can find Chelsea House on the World Wide Web
at http://www.infobaselearning.com.

Text design by Keith Trego
Cover design by Alicia Post
Composition by EJB Publishing Services
Cover printed by Yurchak Printing, Landisville, Pa.
Book printed and bound by Yurchak Printing, Landisville, Pa.
Date printed: June 2011
Printed in the United States of America

10 9 8 7 6 5 4 3 2 1

This book is printed on acid-free paper.

All links and Web addresses were checked and verified to be correct at the time of publication. Because of the dynamic nature of the Web, some addresses and links may have changed since publication and may no longer be valid.

FOREWORD ⦀▷

Alan Marzilli, M.A., J.D.
Birmingham, Alabama

The POINT/COUNTERPOINT series offers the reader a greater understanding of some of the most controversial issues in contemporary American society—issues such as capital punishment, immigration, gay rights, and gun control. We have looked for the most contemporary issues and have included topics—such as the controversies surrounding "blogging"—that we could not have imagined when the series began.

In each volume, the author has selected an issue of particular importance and set out some of the key arguments on both sides of the issue. Why study both sides of the debate? Maybe you have yet to make up your mind on an issue, and the arguments presented in the book will help you to form an opinion. More likely, however, you will already have an opinion on many of the issues covered by the series. There is always the chance that you will change your opinion after reading the arguments for the other side. But even if you are firmly committed to an issue—for example, school prayer or animal rights—reading both sides of the argument will help you to become a more effective advocate for your cause. By gaining an understanding of opposing arguments, you can develop answers to those arguments.

Perhaps more importantly, listening to the other side sometimes helps you see your opponent's arguments in a more human way. For example, Sister Helen Prejean, one of the nation's most visible opponents of capital punishment, has been deeply affected by her interactions with the families of murder victims. By seeing the families' grief and pain, she understands much better why people support the death penalty, and she is able to carry out her advocacy with a greater sensitivity to the needs and beliefs of death penalty supporters.

The books in the series include numerous features that help the reader to gain a greater understanding of the issues. Real-life examples illustrate the human side of the issues. Each chapter also includes excerpts from relevant laws, court cases, and other material, which provide a better foundation for understanding the arguments. The volumes contain citations to relevant sources of law and information, and an appendix guides the reader through the basics of legal research, both on the Internet and in the library. Today, through free Web sites, it is easy to access legal documents, and these books might give you ideas for your own research.

Studying the issues covered by the POINT/COUNTERPOINT series is more than an academic activity. The issues described in the books affect all of us as citizens. They are the issues that today's leaders debate and tomorrow's leaders will decide. While all of the issues covered in the POINT/COUNTERPOINT series are controversial today, and will remain so for the foreseeable future, it is entirely possible that the reader might one day play a central role in resolving the debate. Today it might seem that some debates—such as capital punishment and abortion—will never be resolved.

However, our nation's history is full of debates that seemed as though they never would be resolved, and many of the issues are now well settled—at least on the surface. In the nineteenth century, abolitionists met with widespread resistance to their efforts to end slavery. Ultimately, the controversy threatened the union, leading to the Civil War between the northern and southern states. Today, while a public debate over the merits of slavery would be unthinkable, racism persists in many aspects of society.

Similarly, today nobody questions women's right to vote. Yet at the beginning of the twentieth century, suffragists fought public battles for women's voting rights, and it was not until the passage of the Nineteenth Amendment in 1920 that the legal right of women to vote was established nationwide.

What makes an issue controversial? Often, controversies arise when most people agree that there is a problem but disagree about the best way to solve it. There is little argument that poverty is a major problem in the United States, especially in inner cities and rural areas. Yet, people disagree vehemently about the best way to address the problem. To some, the answer is social programs, such as welfare, food stamps, and public housing. However, many argue that such subsidies encourage dependence on government benefits while unfairly penalizing those who work and pay taxes, and that the real solution is to require people to support themselves.

American society is in a constant state of change, and sometimes modern practices clash with what many consider to be "traditional values," which are often rooted in conservative political views or religious beliefs. Many blame high crime rates, and problems such as poverty, illiteracy, and drug use on the breakdown of the traditional family structure of a married mother and father raising their children. Since the "sexual revolution" of the 1960s and 1970s, sparked in part by the widespread availability of the birth control pill, marriage rates have declined, and the number of children born outside of marriage has increased. The sexual revolution led to controversies over birth control, sex education, and other issues, most prominently abortion. Similarly, the gay rights movement has been challenged as a threat to traditional values. While many gay men and lesbians want to have the same right to marry and raise families as heterosexuals, many politicians and others have challenged gay marriage and adoption as a threat to American society.

Sometimes, new technology raises issues that we have never faced before, and society disagrees about the best solution. Are people free to swap music online, or does this violate the copyright laws that protect songwriters and musicians' ownership of the music that they create? Should scientists use "genetic engineering" to create new crops that are resistant to disease and pests and produce more food, or is it too risky to use a laboratory to create plants that nature never intended? Modern medicine has continued to increase the average lifespan—which is now 77 years, up from under 50 years at the beginning of the twentieth century—but many people are now choosing to die in comfort rather than living with painful ailments in their later years. For doctors, this presents an ethical dilemma: should they allow their patients to die? Should they assist patients in ending their own lives painlessly?

Perhaps the most controversial issues are those that implicate a Constitutional right. The Bill of Rights—the first 10 Amendments to the U.S. Constitution—spells out some of the most fundamental rights that distinguish our democracy from other nations with fewer freedoms. However, the sparsely worded document is open to interpretation, with each side saying that the Constitution is on their side. The Bill of Rights was meant to protect individual liberties; however, the needs of some individuals clash with society's needs. Thus, the Constitution often serves as a battleground between individuals and government officials seeking to protect society in some way. The First Amendment's guarantee of "freedom of speech" leads to some very difficult questions. Some forms of expression—such as burning an American flag—lead to public outrage, but are protected by the First Amendment. Other types of expression that most people find objectionable—such as child pornography—are not protected by the Constitution. The question is not only where to draw the line, but whether drawing lines around constitutional rights threatens our liberty.

The Bill of Rights raises many other questions about individual rights and societal "good." Is a prayer before a high school football game an "establishment of religion" prohibited by the First Amendment? Does the Second Amendment's promise of "the right to bear arms" include concealed handguns? Does stopping and frisking someone standing on a known drug corner constitute "unreasonable search and seizure" in violation of the Fourth Amendment? Although the U.S. Supreme Court has the ultimate authority in interpreting the U.S. Constitution, its answers do not always satisfy the public. When a group of nine people—sometimes by a five-to-four vote—makes a decision that affects hundreds of millions of others, public outcry can be expected. For example, the Supreme Court's 1973 ruling in *Roe v. Wade* that abortion is protected by the Constitution did little to quell the debate over abortion.

Whatever the root of the controversy, the books in the Point/ Counterpoint series seek to explain to the reader the origins of the debate, the current state of the law, and the arguments on either side of the debate. Our hope in creating this series is that readers will be better informed about the issues facing not only our politicians, but all of our nation's citizens, and become more actively involved in resolving these debates, as voters, concerned citizens, journalists, or maybe even elected officials.

This volume examines some of the controversies surrounding the nation's approach to enforcing its narcotics laws. A growing number of states no longer consider marijuana possession to be criminal, although the federal government still does. All jurisdictions impose criminal penalties for possessing cocaine, heroin, and synthetic drugs such as ecstasy and methamphetamine, as well as the possession of certain drugs like painkillers and sedatives without a prescription. Although many people argue that marijuana has some beneficial medicinal uses, there are fewer such arguments in favor of possession of "harder" drugs like cocaine or heroin. Nevertheless, some argue that the way our society enforces its laws against these substances is counterproductive. Our prisons are overflowing, and a disproportionate percentage of certain demographic groups are behind bars. Many question whether too many people have been jailed rather than given help in avoiding drug addiction. Drug courts are supposed to help in this area, but their effectiveness is open to debate. Also controversial are laws that impose lesser penalties for powder cocaine than "crack" cocaine, which gained a foothold in lower-income neighborhoods with high minority populations. Discussed in this volume are these two controversies relating to the fairness of criminal enforcement, as well as the broader question of whether marijuana should be illegal at all.

An Overview of the War on Drugs

In the early part of the twentieth century, the U.S. government waged war against the ravaging abuses of alcohol—a substance that some alleged corrupted morals and degraded society. Temperance unions, politicians, and others railed against the excesses of alcohol. This outcry culminated in a national policy known as Prohibition. The Eighteenth Amendment outlawed the sale and manufacture of all alcoholic beverages in 1920.

Prohibition was a disaster, leading to all sorts of illegal bootlegging, government corruption, and hypocritical government conduct. In his 2010 book *Lies the Government Told You,* Judge Andrew Napolitano reports that "there was a great deal of corruption and violence caused by the government's ban."[1] The result was that in 1933 Congress and the states approved the Twenty-first Amendment, which repealed the Eighteenth Amendment. It is the only time in American history that one constitutional amendment superseded another one.

Though this amendment declared an end to Prohibition, the nation did not remain silent with respect to drugs. The federal government passed the Marihuana Tax Act of 1937, which essentially drove marijuana production underground. The head of the Internal Revenue Service (IRS), Marion Allen, announced that everyone would have to pay a serious tax on the sale of marijuana, cannabis, and hemp.[2] The *Washington Post* referred to the problem as the "marijuana menace," saying that many people in society were becoming addicted to this dangerous substance.[3] In 1938, the attorney general of Kansas proclaimed that the drug was "more dangerous than cocaine or opium, neither of which will grow in this country."[4] Later that year authorities in Philadelphia banned a film about marijuana in the city.[5]

The 1960s and 1970s, however, brought concerns about a wide range of drugs far beyond marijuana, as illegal drug use became much more common. The *New York Times* reported in 1965 that many young people went from smoking marijuana to taking heroin.[6] Governor Nelson Rockefeller of New York declared that the problem was so serious that a large influx of state and federal money was needed to fight the addiction problem of various narcotics.[7]

President Richard Nixon declared a "war" on drugs in the early 1970s because of a wave of crime in the late 1960s associated with an increase in the use of heroin.[8] In 1971, Nixon called drug abuse "public enemy number one." In the 1970s and 1980s, a different drug—cocaine—ravaged parts of the country. A much harder drug than marijuana, cocaine involved major smuggling in areas such as Miami, Florida; and parts of California. In 1973, a House of Representatives report declared that at least $5 billion was needed to combat a drug "epidemic" in the nation's schools.[9]

During her husband's time in the White House, First Lady Nancy Reagan became well-known for her campaign against drug abuse. Here, she and *Good Morning America* host David Hartman discuss youth drug abuse problems in the show's New York studio on October 12, 1983. During the program, they interviewed former drug abusers who had kicked the habit and Vice President George H.W. Bush, who was then heading President Ronald Reagan's drug smuggling task force.

In 1982, President Ronald Reagan—partly in response to the threat from increasing cocaine use—more forcefully declared a "war on drugs." An unprecedented amount of federal and state resources was aimed at illegal drugs. First Lady Nancy Reagan joined in the process with her much publicized "Just Say No" antidrug campaign.

In June 1986, tragedy struck when star college basketball player Len Bias died of a cocaine overdose on the eve of his fulfilling his dream of becoming a professional basketball player in the NBA. Bias's death spurred lawmakers to get even tougher on illegal drugs.

The continual support for the "war on drugs" led to an increase in American law enforcement efforts in curtailing the

---

THE LETTER OF THE LAW

Excerpts from the United States Constitution

Eighteenth Amendment

Section 1. After one year from the ratification of this article the manufacture, sale, or transportation of intoxicating liquors within, the importation thereof into, or the exportation thereof from the United States and all territory subject to the jurisdiction thereof for beverage purposes is hereby prohibited.

Section 2. The Congress and the several States shall have concurrent power to enforce this article by appropriate legislation.

Section 3. This article shall be inoperative unless it shall have been ratified as an amendment to the Constitution by the legislatures of the several States, as provided in the Constitution, within seven years from the date of the submission hereof to the States by the Congress.

Twenty-first Amendment

Section 1. The eighteenth article of amendment to the Constitution of the United States is hereby repealed.

Section 2. The transportation or importation into any State, Territory, or possession of the United States for delivery or use therein of intoxicating liquors, in violation of the laws thereof, is hereby prohibited.

Section 3. This article shall be inoperative unless it shall have been ratified as an amendment to the Constitution by conventions in the several States, as provided in the Constitution, within seven years from the date of the submission hereof to the States by the Congress.

drug trade. The results were mixed, however, and criticism persisted. In the 1980s, the government found a new target in the form of crack cocaine, a smokeable, cheaper form of powder cocaine. The severity of this drug's epidemic forced legislators to change federal law to allow much greater sentences proportionally for those charged with offenses involving crack cocaine than for those charged with offenses involving powder cocaine.

This change in the law resulted in many more arrests and greater imprisonment of drug offenders. Law professor Steven B. Duke reports that nearly a half million people are in American prisons because of drug-related offenses.[10] Law student Jennifer Broxmeyer writes: "The War on Drugs has played no small part in creating what is now the largest prison population in the world, with more than one in one hundred American adults behind bars."[11]

Another systemic problem with the war on drugs is police corruption. Much as there was serious corruption in law enforcement during Prohibition, many assert that there are continuing problems associated with police corruption. "It goes on and on," Duke writes. "A federal investigation of New York City police in 2004 bagged a dozen police who were stealing drugs and money from drug dealers."[12]

Summary

Three controversial issues related to the drug war will be examined here. The first debates the effectiveness of drug courts. Should those charged with drug crimes be prosecuted criminally and warehoused in a penal institution, particularly in this age of mass incarceration? Today, more people than ever before are contending that alternatives to the traditional criminal justice method are needed. One alternative is a drug-treatment court, usually reserved as an option for those nonviolent offenders who are convicted of drug charges. Supporters contend that drug courts offer a realistic alternative to mass incarceration and help to break the cycle of jail time for those addicted to drugs.

Opponents counter that drug courts do not really work and represent a failed solution.

The second issue to be discussed concerns the sentencing of those charged with crack-cocaine drug offenses. This issue has been raging in legal circles since the mid-1980s. In 1986, the U.S. Congress passed a law, the Anti-Drug Abuse Act of 1986, which provided for much greater sentences for those charged with offenses involving cocaine base—commonly called crack cocaine (which is one type of cocaine base)—as opposed to powder cocaine. The sentencing disparity was 100 to 1, meaning that an

Radio Address of President Ronald Reagan

In the next few days we'll announce the administration's new strategy for the prevention of drug abuse and drug trafficking. . . . For too long the people in Washington took the attitude that the drug problem was so large nothing could be done about it. Well, we don't accept this sit-on-your-hands kind of thinking. We've decided to do more than pay lip service to the problem, and we started where narcotics crime was the worst: South Florida.

This garden spot had turned into a battlefield for competing drug pushers who were terrorizing Florida's citizens. I established a task force under Vice President [George H.W.] Bush's leadership to help the citizens of South Florida fight back. As part of a coordinated plan, we beefed up the number of judges, prosecutors, and law enforcement people. We used military radar and intelligence to detect drug traffickers, which, until we changed the law, could not be done. We increased efforts overseas to cut drugs off before they left other countries' borders.

Well, the results of our task force have been dramatic. The vice president tells me drug-related arrests are up over 40 percent, the amount of marijuana seized is up about 80 percent, and the amount of cocaine seized has more than doubled. The important thing is we're hurting the traffickers. It's true that when we close off one place they can move somewhere else. But one thing is different now: We're going to be waiting for them. . . .

individual with 5 grams of crack cocaine was treated the same as someone with 500 grams of powder cocaine.

Opponents contend that this ratio, which has been reduced by recent federal legislation, calls into question the underlying fairness of the criminal justice system. They contend that the law unfairly impacts African-American citizens. Supporters of the law counter that the intent was not to punish certain offenders but merely to provide protection from those who traffic in crack cocaine, a drug associated with more violence than powder cocaine.

The strategy I just received will help us duplicate the South Florida experience for the entire United States. . . . We're not just going to let them go somewhere else; we're going to be on their tail.

Now, you probably wonder why I'm so optimistic. Well, for the first time, the actions of the different government agencies and departments dealing with narcotics are being coordinated. There are 9 departments and 33 agencies of government that have some responsibility in the drug area, but until now, the activities of these agencies were not being coordinated. . . . Now, for the very first time, the federal government is waging a planned, concerted campaign.

Previous administrations had drug strategies, but they didn't have the structure to carry them out. We now have that structure.

In addition to the enforcement element, our strategy will also focus on international cooperation, education, and prevention . . . [as well as] detoxification and treatment and research.

The mood toward drugs is changing in this country, and the momentum is with us. We're making no excuses for drugs—hard, soft, or otherwise. Drugs are bad, and we're going after them. As I've said before, we've taken down the surrender flag and run up the battle flag. And we're going to win the war on drugs.

Source: Ronald Reagan, "Radio Address to the Nation on Federal Drug Policy," October 2, 1982. http://www.presidency.ucsb.edu/ws/index.php?pid=43085.

The third issue debated here concerns the legalization of marijuana. Supporters contend that marijuana has many positive medical uses, while opponents counter that marijuana remains a menace and has many deleterious impacts.

Drug Courts Reduce Crime, Cut Costs, and Save Lives

Dan Tousignant lived a dangerous life as a self-admitted "meth-head," addicted to the drug methamphetamine. He robbed, stole, and criminalized others to feed his drug habit. He was going nowhere good until he came in contact with a drug court in Ramsey County, Minnesota. The drug-court program was not easy. "Believe me, this is the toughest thing I've done in my life," Tousignant told the *St. Paul Pioneer Press*, but in May 2010, he became the one-hundredth graduate of the program.[1]

Heather Bower developed such a serious drug habit that she was paying $1,500 a week to feed it. Often she resorted to criminal activity, including forgery, to be able to buy illegal drugs. Law enforcement officials in Florida arrested her more than 25 times. She finally began to turn the corner when she entered Circuit Judge Linda Babb's Treatment Court. Now finished with the program, she plans to be a drug counselor.[2]

John Wedel faced arrest and jail time for possession of methamphetamine. Life looked bleak until he received help from the Douglas County Drug Court in Oklahoma. Wedel graduated from drug court and has been sober for more than nine months. "It was a long haul, but I'm grateful for it," he told the *Omaha World-Herald*. "It saved my life."[3]

Emily Weir had a substance-abuse problem, getting arrested four times for alcohol-related offenses starting at age 16. Then, she received the help she needed after being placed in a county drug court in Michigan. She got her life together and became a nursing student at Eastern Michigan University.[4]

Emily Hoeffner faced a similar situation. A recovering heroin addict, she had robbed her drug dealer to get high. She received her second chance with the Youth Offender Court in Las Vegas, Nevada. "Some people don't get another chance," she said. "They either OD, lose everything, end up on the streets or end up in prison. I get another chance."[5]

Tousignant, Bower, Wedel, Weir, and Hoeffner are not alone. They are among thousands who have been given a second opportunity at life, the chance to reverse their fortunes and beat dangerous drug addictions. The one thing they all have in common is the fact that drug courts intervened to stop their downward spirals. There are more than 2,500 drug courts operating in the United States today. The first was established in 1989 in Dade County, Florida, with Judge Stanley Goldstein's "Diversion and Treatment Program." Something had to be done in Miami, as the city had been besieged by a cocaine and crack-cocaine epidemic. Under this program, which was approved by the Dade County state attorney Janet Reno (who later became U.S. attorney general under President Bill Clinton), many people charged with drug crimes were moved into the drug court rather than the more traditional criminal court.[6]

At the time Goldstein seemed to be an unlikely choice to run the nation's first drug court, as he had begun his career

In this September 25, 2009, photo, Superior Court Judge Jack Burchard talks to Kristina Gipson, in Okanogan, Washington. If all goes according to plan, Gipson will graduate from the state's drug court program.

as a police officer and had a reputation as a very tough judge. As a police officer, he worked as a motorcycle cop, in street patrol, and in other areas. He then graduated from law school and spent two years as a prosecutor before becoming a criminal defense attorney. When Circuit Judge Gerald Wetherington and Circuit Judge Herb Klein created the concept of a drug court, they pegged Goldstein as the person to handle the first one. "Because of his background, being a cop and a criminal defense attorney, nobody was going to blow any smoke past him," Wetherington said. "He was going to be tough when he had to be tough, but he also had a very kind and caring heart."[7]

Goldstein, however, was not convinced at first, telling the *Miami Herald*: "You're never going to get anybody off crack cocaine that way. They've got to come to you when they're ready."[8] Later, Goldstein became the biggest supporter of drug courts, as he began to see more and more people turn their lives around in a positive direction. He recalled that the best testament to the work of the drug court came from one man who went through drug court, as well as the man's mother. The man, having faced multiple arrests, graduated from the program and regained his personal and professional success. "He even hired five people from the program to work for him," Judge Goldstein said.[9]

The best confirmation of the program, however, came from the man's mother, who wrote Goldstein a letter that said in part: "Judge, you have given me my life back."[10] Goldstein had such an indelible impact on the drug-court movement that there is now a Stanley M. Goldstein Drug Court Hall of Fame, which honors distinguished drug-court practitioners.

In 1989, Goldstein's drug court was the only one in the nation. A second followed in Multnomah County, Oregon. As of December 2010, there are more than 2,500 drug courts in the United States. They help more than 70,000 individuals nationwide. Some focus on juveniles, others on adults. Each offers a real chance at improving the criminal justice system by keeping nonviolent drug users out of the system. They give people second chances but do not give them a free pass. In general, drug courts offer a combination of counseling and treatment, probation, and court appearances. A judge closely monitors a defendant's progress, including drug tests. If the defendant slips up and tests positive, the defendant may be removed from the drug-court program and processed into the regular court system to face stiff jail time.[11]

Drug courts reduce crime.

Drug courts help individuals turn their lives around and turn away from crime. How so? If the traditional criminal justice system locks up a drug defendant, the strong likelihood exists that he or she will relapse when released from prison. But, if the criminal justice system can treat the addiction via drug courts, the former drug defendant has no need to commit a crime to obtain illegal drugs.

Studies have shown that individuals who participate in and graduate from drug-court programs have a greater chance to turn away from crime. This means that the recidivism rate for those in drug-court programs is better than for those who simply enter the traditional criminal justice system. Reducing crime may be the most important aspect of drug courts, because drug offenders are the most likely type of offender to re-offend. Drugs are addictive, and individuals often spend much of their lives trying to break the terrible cycle of addiction.

QUOTABLE

John K. Roman, senior researcher at the Urban Institute's Justice Policy Center

We found that drug-court participants self-report significantly less criminal behavior than the comparison group. During the 18-month tracking period, for instance, the total number of criminal acts was reduced by 52 percent. The reductions in offending persisted throughout the observation period, even after most in the treatment group had left drug court.

We also found that significantly fewer drug-court participants self-reported drug use than in the comparison group. Finally, we found that drug courts are cost-effective. The average net benefit to society is about $4,000 per drug-court participant, regardless of how well that participant did in drug court....

We estimate the United States spends slightly more than half a billion dollars to treat drug-court clients each year. This investment yields more than $1 billion in annual savings, which is more than $2 in benefits for every $1 in costs.

Source: Testimony of John K. Roman, Domestic Policy Subcommittee, Oversight and Government Reform Committee, U.S. House of Representatives, July 22, 2010. http://www. urban.org/uploadedpdf/901371-drug-courts-pre-trial-diversion.pdf.

A study in California found that the re-arrest rate of drug-court participants was 29 percent, while the re-arrest rate for those not in the program was more than 40 percent. A study of drug courts in Suffolk County, Massachusetts, determined that drug-court participants were 13 percent less likely to be arrested again.[12]

A 10-year study of the Drug Court of Multnomah County, Oregon—the second oldest drug court in the United States— revealed clear results of the positive impact of drug courts on reducing crime. The study found that "the Drug Court significantly reduced the incidence and frequency of criminal recidivism for participants compared to offenders who did not participate."[13] This study determined that the re-arrest rate for drug-court participants dropped by nearly 30 percent.[14] It further determined that the results were good for at least 14 years.[15]

Judge Don Ash has presided over a drug court in Murfreesboro, Tennessee, for more than 10 years. He says the impact on his circuit court has been indelible. "Fifty percent of the participants who start drug court graduate, and our recidivism rate is less than 20 percent," he said in a personal interview. "If I send someone to prison, the recidivism rate is over 60 percent."[16]

Lisa Murkowski, a U.S. senator from Alaska, stated that "in Alaska, the drug courts have been models in reducing recidivism—13 percent for those who have graduated from the programs as compared with 32 percent for offenders who didn't participate."[17]

Drug courts represent a real change in the criminal justice system. They give the system a chance to do more than simply throw more offenders in jail. Locking up inmates is only a short-term solution that is no solution at all. "Drug courts really are central to reducing drug abuse and to keeping communities safe," said Laurie Robinson, assistant U.S. attorney general, to a coalition of state drug court coordinators in September 2010. "But I think the real contribution of drug courts . . . is that they've introduced a new way of thinking about the justice system."[18]

Drug courts reduce costs.

Numerous studies confirm that drug courts reduce overall costs to the justice system. It costs far more to warehouse inmates than to get them into treatment and out of the illegal drug cycle. "It costs $5,000 a year to have an addict in drug court, while if I put the same individual in jail, it costs $35,000 annually and they receive no treatment for their addiction," Judge Don Ash said.[19] A study in one Illinois county concluded that it cost $2,000 a year to send a person through drug court compared with $23,800 a year to incarcerate that individual.[20]

The Urban Institute's Justice Policy Center engaged in an extensive study of various drug courts and their participants

QUOTABLE

Gil Kerlikowske, director of the Office of National Drug Control Policy

Unfortunately, those who are addicted to drugs often interface with the criminal justice system, either primarily or secondarily, due to their addiction. This must be treated as an opportunity. Addressing drug abuse at every point in the criminal/ juvenile justice spectrum—beginning with law enforcement, through adjudication, into correctional facilities, and back into communities through the re-entry process—is imperative to breaking the cycle of substance abuse and associated criminal behavior. With nearly 50 percent of jail and prison inmates meeting clinical criteria for abuse or addiction, the justice system can play a significant role not only in protecting citizens from crime, but also in reducing substance abuse through the expansion of drug courts and other problem-solving courts, re-entry programs, and treatment programs within correctional facilities.

Source: Testimony of Gil Kerlikowske, Domestic Policy Subcommittee, Oversight and Government Reform Committee, U.S. House of Representatives, May 19, 2009. http://www.wilsoncenter.org/news/docs/051909_dpc_subcommittee.pdf.

over an 18-month tracking period. In the study more than 5,000 offenders were interviewed and information was collected on participants in 23 drug courts in 8 states. The study found that drug courts were very cost-effective, saving at least $4,000 per participant.[21]

The National Center for Policy Analysis reviewed the literature on drug courts and costs, concluding: "Given the success of drug courts, and the projected savings if more programs were implemented, the United States should use drug courts to save taxpayers' money and effectively treat criminals with drug problems."[22]

Summary

Numerous studies confirm that drug courts save lives, reduce crime, and cut costs. If drug courts were not a success, they would not have grown from zero in 1988 to more than 2,500 nationwide. More and more judges, scholars, attorneys, and social workers believe that they are necessary to combat the insidious spread of drug abuse and crime. Anecdotally, many individuals once mired in drug addiction have credited drug courts with turning their lives around. Lives have been saved, families have been reunited, and countless people have been protected from becoming crime victims.

Studies have shown that those who participate and complete drug-court programs are less likely to turn to crime. Furthermore, the cost of treating someone in a drug-court program is far less than keeping him or her in jail or prison. More efforts are being made to increase the number of juvenile courts and other so-called problem-solving courts, such as family dependency treatment courts, re-entry drug courts, and DWI courts specifically for impaired drivers.[23]

"Research verifies that no other justice intervention can rival the results produced by drug courts," says a report produced by the National Drug Court Institute. "Drug courts are demonstratively effective. According to over a decade of research, drug courts significantly improve substance abuse treatment outcomes, substantially reduce crime, and produce greater cost benefits than any other justice strategy."[24]

Drug Courts Do Not Work and Create Problems

An individual gets arrested for a drug crime. It is his third offense, but fortunately his first two offenses were nonviolent misdemeanors. This time, however, the prosecutor means business. This time the individual is looking at serious jail time. His defense attorney tells him that he has another alternative—to convince the trial judge that he wants to get clean and undergo drug treatment. Only then, the judge might take pity on the man and divert him to drug court.

The individual knows this is his chance to beat the system and avoid jail time again. He goes before the judge and says with all sincerity that he is committed to turning his life around, even though he just wants to go to drug court to avoid jail. But he convinces the trial court judge that his desire to change is genuine. His time in drug court begins with promise, but soon his obsession with drugs continues and he re-offends. He breaks his promises and tests positive for drugs. He does not graduate from drug court, serves out his sentence, and then goes back out on the streets to commit more crimes.

Another man really desires to turn his life around and turn away from drug use. He wants a second chance at life, realizing that he has been headed down the wrong path for a long time. Unfortunately, he has a prior conviction for robbery, as he held up someone to get money to buy drugs. The drug-court administrator denies him entrance into the program because of the armed robbery conviction. The administrator thinks, "We can't have anyone in this program with a violent felony conviction. Those individuals generally are not suitable for treatment."

While these two examples are fictional, they are based on real-life events. Drug courts often do not work, as many individuals who are sent to them fail to complete treatment. An even more disturbing problem is that the selection process for who actually gets to enter drug court is fundamentally flawed and frequently biased. Too often, drug courts do not operate fairly and accept those individuals most deserving of help. So why are so many drug courts in existence? Morris Hoffman, a legal commentator and trial court judge in Colorado, describes their growth as "the hysteria of drug courts."[1]

Drug courts do not work.

The dirty secret surrounding drug courts is their low success rate. Hoffman concluded in a law review article that drug courts simply do not work. Although many kinds of studies have examined drug courts, not one unbiased account has demonstrated with any degree of reliability that drug courts are beneficial to society. Perhaps the most startling aspect of the drug-court phenomenon is that drug courts have so quickly become fixtures of our jurisprudence, or our system of law, in the absence of satisfying empirical evidence that they actually serve some legitimate purpose.

There have been studies that tout the successes of drug courts, but these reports are flawed because the creators of the studies are pro-drug court. Nonbiased studies confirm that claims of success by drug courts are often exaggerated. Researcher Elizabeth Ann Green examined the numbers behind the nation's first drug court in Dade County, Florida, in 1991. Her study found that 25 percent of those assigned to drug court were arrested for felonies at a rate 5 percent higher than those not assigned to drug court. She also found that only about 20 percent of those in drug court actually graduated. Green, who was director of criminal justice operations for the Dade courts, candidly wrote that the "findings indicate that the Drug Court is a success in some respects and a failure in others."[2] Similarly,

QUOTABLE

Judge Morris Hoffman

Drug courts don't work, and never have. They don't reduce recidivism or relapse. Instead, they trigger such massive net widening that they end up sending many more drug defendants to prison than traditional criminal courts ever did. Their failures have resulted in a quiet refocusing, from pre-adjudicative treatment to post-adjudicative treatment. That is, they have become officially what they have always been unofficially: a form of glorified, and terribly expensive, probation. Their continued popularity is a testament not to their effectiveness but rather to their political appeal, and to the irrational commitment of a handful of true believers. Federal courts should continue to resist them.

What is most disturbing about the drug court movement is that we have been down this rehabilitative road before, and have apparently not learned anything from the spectacular failures of the rehabilitative model. It not only didn't work, it invested the judicial branch with dangerous powers we eventually decided were not acceptable in a democratic society. Now it's déjà vu all over again. Drug courts don't work, and they have created a dangerous psycho-judicial branch populated by judges who think they are doctors, who think drug addiction is a treatable disease, and who send their patients to prison when they fail to respond to treatment.

Source: Morris Hoffman, "The Rehabilitative Ideal and the Drug Court Reality," 14 *Federal Sentencing Reporter* 172, 172–173 (2001).

the American Bar Association conducted a study of the Dade County drug court and a few other early drug courts. The study found that the recidivism rate was nearly identical for those who were drug-court defendants and those who were not drug-court defendants.[3]

Many studies purport to show that there is a reduction in recidivism among those who attend and graduate from drug courts, but these studies are methodologically flawed. Many studies failed to select target group members randomly. In 2006, one surveyor of various drug-court studies proclaimed that the results were "maddeningly inconclusive." He concluded:

> So after thirteen years of operations of hundreds of drug courts across the country, and with unprecedented motives and opportunities to demonstrate their effectiveness, the quality and strength of the evidence of drug court effectiveness is no better today than it was in 1993. Most studies are deeply flawed, and the ones that are not do not justify the conclusion that drug courts are having any demonstrable impact on either recidivism or relapse.[4]

Even some people who support drug courts in theory recognize that there is less than sterling evidence that drug courts actually work and reduce recidivism rates over the long haul. A 2009 study reported:

> While it is generally accepted that drug courts effectively reduce rearrest rates relative to simple probation or incarceration, there is some reason to be cautious when interpreting these results. Some studies show little or no impact from drug court participation and it can be difficult to specify which components of the program or the research design may be contributing to these results.[5]

The National Association of Criminal Defense Lawyers (NACDL) reported that drug courts "cause problems and engender disparities in many areas, including the admission process, the role and ethical obligations of defense counsel, and the misguided use of limited public resources."[6]

Proponents of drug courts emphasize success stories—those individuals who actually benefit from drug court and manage to turn their lives around. There are, however, many more individuals who failed to complete their programs or were not helped by their time in drug courts. NACDL writes in its September 2009 report that "it is incontrovertible that for every person who graduates from drug court, others did not qualify or did not complete the program."[7]

A study in Scotland evaluated the country's drug courts, which were based on the U.S. model. The results were disturbing, as recidivism continued and little progress was made. Instead, most drug-court defendants failed to graduate and many re-offended within a short period of time. Commentator Stanton Peele says the Scottish study is indicative of the systemic failure of drug courts in the United States:

> Instead of learning how to deal better with their lives, drug users learn fictive explanations for their behavior and destructive theories of substance abuse and addiction. . . . In the United States, especially, these explanations focus on drug abuse as a disease users supposedly have.[8]

Drug courts are not operating fairly.

Drug courts often cater to white defendants and those with more money. Dr. Peter Banys, who works in substance-abuse treatment, has admitted that "many drug courts skim. They . . . have exclusion criteria to pick people who are more likely to do well."[9] Another has stated bluntly: "I've been to drug courts where I have seen not one client of color."[10]

Some drug courts exclude anyone who has been convicted of a violent felony. Others exclude anyone who has any sort of felony conviction. Still others exclude those with evidence of mental illness or those with a domestic violence problem. NACDL reports:

> The criteria and process for admission into drug court are guided largely by tough-on-crime politics, focusing on first-time or nonviolent offenders, with little consideration of smart-on-crime approaches that target those most in need of intensive treatment who would otherwise spend a long time in prison.[11]

Drug courts need to focus on those most in need of treatment, whether their record is favorable or not. NACDL writes, "Every defendant who needs treatment should be presumed eligible for a drug court program."[12] Drug courts should not favor certain socioeconomic groups or those of specific racial categories. Too many people are excluded unfairly.[13]

Some evidence indicates that drug courts exacerbate racial disparities in the criminal justice system with respect to minorities, particularly African-American defendants. Marquette law school professor Michael O'Hear identifies several reasons for this disturbing phenomenon. First, drug courts do nothing about racial disparities in arrest patterns. Second, many drug courts have strict eligibility requirements that disqualify those with a longer arrest pattern. Because the criminal justice system leads to more incarceration per capita for blacks, many African Americans are excluded from participation. Third, drug-court programs have a high failure rate, and African Americans have a higher failing rate because of their typically lower socioeconomic status limits their opportunities for successful treatment.[14] O'Hear reports that "failure rates are higher for blacks than whites, by thirty or more percentage points in some DTCs [drug treatment courts]."[15] In fact, O'Hear bluntly states that "no court-based diversion program is likely to make a large dent in the racial disparities that plague our criminal justice system."[16]

Drug courts simply lead to more drug arrests.

Morris Hoffman, a state trial court judge in Denver, contends that drug courts are counterproductive in part because they cause the police to arrest more people for drug crimes. He notes, "They have the perverse effect of sending more drug defendants to prison, because their poor treatment results get swamped by an increase in the number of drug arrests."[17]

Hoffman claims that in Denver, drug arrests shot up exponentially after the city resorted to drug courts: "At the end of those two years, we were sending almost twice the number of drug defendants to prison than we did before drug court."[18] Researchers for the Sentencing Project conclude:

> Of great concern is the contention that drug courts could be increasing the number of people arrested for drug crimes, instead of decreasing in the long term the number of people processed in the criminal justice system. Research has not yet focused on determining whether drug court participants would have ended up in the criminal justice system if not for the drug court.[19]

Judges are trained in the law, not drug treatment. Therefore, the proper people to consider drug treatment for addicts should be highly trained health-care specialists, not judges who are trained in the criminal law code. It is a question of apples and oranges. Unfortunately, some well-meaning judges attempt to serve dual roles, and this simply does not work with respect to drug courts.

Judges sometimes get quite upset when a drug-court defendant fails a drug test or otherwise fails to comply with the directives of the program. The judge then sentences the drug-court defendant to more time in prison under the traditional criminal justice model than he or she would have received under the treatment model. This presents a fundamental question of fairness.[20] The study by the Sentencing Project points out:

> Because most individuals who enter drug court are convicted of non-violent offenses, many would have experienced short, if any, periods in jail. Participants who are punished with sanctions sometimes end up with multiple stays in jail.[21]

Drug courts do not help those most in need.

Perhaps the strongest mark against drug courts is that they often cannot help those individuals most in need of drug treatment—the hard-core addict whose addiction has led him or her to commit many crimes, including felonies. Thus, many of these individuals may never pass the eligibility requirements for drug-court admission. Researchers admit that "persons using more serious drugs and with the most severe addiction problems may be left out of drug court programs because of their criminal history."[22] They add that "the question remains then, as to whether those who graduate drug court treatment tend to be those with less serious addictions, while those with significant addiction problems end up in jail?"[23]

Moreover, many of these hard-core drug addicts are more susceptible to relapse. This makes sense because their addictions may be more severe and have endured for a longer period of time. If a judge revokes a person's participation in drug court after a first or second violation, then the person will not benefit from drug court. In part, this problem is understandable, because some hard-core drug addicts and criminals may try to game the system. That is, they may try to feign that they will go clean and go to drug court in order to avoid another stint in prison. On the other hand, if the criminal justice system really cares about rehabilitation and helping people, should not its focus be on those most in need of treatment? All of the problems with the drug-court system clearly show that treating serious drug addiction should be handled outside the criminal justice system and not within it.

Summary

Drug courts seem like a good idea and are supported by many well-meaning individuals. It sounds good to reduce overcrowded prisons and get people the treatment they need to address their underlying addictions. The problem, though, is that these drug courts do not work; in fact, they create even more problems. There is a great failure rate in existing drug treatment courts. Studies have shown that there is still a large recidivism rate for those who complete drug-court programs. Law professor Michael O'Hear cautions that "the turn to drug courts carries with it sufficient risks and costs that their superiority over traditional law enforcement approaches should not be taken for granted."[24]

Drug courts also have exclusionary policies with respect to who is admitted to the programs. They tend to favor those with reduced criminal sentences and no violent behavior or violent crimes on their records. Yet the question remains: Are not those with serious criminal histories associated with drug abuse the individuals who *most* need treatment?

Drug courts also exacerbate racial disparities in the criminal justice system, or at the very least, do nothing to address these disturbing disparities. Finally, drug courts also do not work because judges, not being trained in medicine, do not have the skills and experience to serve as drug-treatment professionals. As Hoffman writes:

> By simultaneously treating drug use as a crime and as a disease, without coming to grips with the inherent

contradictions of those two approaches, drug courts are not satisfying either the legitimate and compassionate interests of the treatment community or the legitimate and rational interests of the law enforcement community.[25]

The Sentencing Disparity Between Crack and Powder Cocaine Should Be Eliminated

Stephanie Nodd, an African-American woman, has spent much of her life behind bars. This native of Mobile, Alabama, quit high school in the ninth grade after becoming pregnant. She had to drop out of school to take care of her infant child. At age 20, she met a young, charismatic drug dealer who promised her a better way of life. Although she was involved with the drug scene and did help him set up some drug deals, she was by no means the ringleader.

Prosecutors, however, charged her as the manager of a crack-cocaine distribution operation. Convicted and sentenced to 30 years in prison in 1990, she will not be released until late 2016. In prison, she earned her GED and has taken many college-level courses. Her mother died while she was incarcerated, and her young daughter is now an adult. For her youthful indiscretions in helping a drug dealer, Nodd has spent her adult life behind bars. In fact, she received a much greater sentence than the drug dealer whom she assisted.[1]

DeJarion Echols faced a similar fate when he sold crack cocaine as a teenager to help pay his way through college. The police searched his apartment and found 44 grams of crack cocaine. They charged him, however, with distributing nearly 500 grams, believing that constituted the accurate amount of Echols's illegal transactions with the drug. They also charged him with a gun offense. He pleaded guilty to the drug and weapon charges, receiving two 10-year sentences. Echols went to prison, leaving behind a wife and two young daughters. The sentencing judge, Walter Tyler, reluctantly imposed the mandatory minimum sentences, though he believed them too harsh. "This is one of those situations where I'd like to see a congressman sitting before me," he said.[2] Echols has tried his best to improve himself in prison, taking and passing numerous courses. Yet he will not see his family until he is in his mid-forties.

Sadly, Nodd and Echols are not isolated incidents or outliers. They represent a class of individuals who have fallen victim to an unfair system of punishment. This system disproportionately and disparately punishes individuals charged and convicted of crack-cocaine offenses.

There is a dubious distinction between crack- and powder-cocaine sentences.

How did we get to such a disparity? In the 1980s, prosecutors in drug cases relied on the "expert" testimony of a police investigator named Johnny St. Valentine Brown Jr., who claimed he had a doctorate in pharmacology from Howard University. Brown, who often explained the damaging aspects of drugs in colorful terms, served as a witness in more than 1,000 drug cases. Congress later called on Brown for advice when passing a new antidrug law. Brown testified that 20 grams of crack cocaine was as bad or worse than 1,000 grams of powder cocaine. Congress relied in part on Brown's testimony in coming up with the

Cocaine, seen here in its white powder form, is obtained from the leaves of the coca plant. Cultivation, possession, and distribution of cocaine are illegal in virtually all parts of the world. Despite being severely penalized in almost every country, the worldwide use of cocaine remains widespread, particularly in industrialized nations like the United States.

Anti-Drug Abuse Act of 1986. Under this law, defendants with five grams of crack cocaine were considered the same as defendants with 500 grams of powder cocaine.[3]

A defense attorney later proved that Brown had lied about his credentials. He did not have a doctorate in pharmacology and really had no scientific basis for his exaggerated claim that a few grams of crack cocaine were worse than hundreds of grams of powder cocaine. It had all been made up. Brown later pleaded guilty after being indicted on several counts of perjury. He was sentenced to a year in prison.[4]

For many years an individual who was caught with 5 grams of crack cocaine would be subject to a criminal sentence of five years in prison. It would take an individual possessing 500 grams of powder cocaine to receive that same five-year imprisonment. Congress came up with five reasons for its support of this 100-to-1 ratio:

(1) crack cocaine was more addictive;
(2) crack cocaine was associated with more violence;
(3) crack cocaine posed risks to children and pregnant women;
(4) crack cocaine was more popular among young people;
(5) crack cocaine's low cost made it more widespread and more likely to be consumed in larger quantities.[5]

This 100-to-1 ratio struck many in the legal community as not only grossly unfair but also racially biased, as minorities typically used crack cocaine more frequently than whites. The Anti-Drug Abuse Act was enacted at the height of the drug-war phenomenon in the mid-1980s. This type of unfair sentencing imprisoned large segments of the poor urban community and exacerbated racial tensions in America. Since 1995, the United States Sentencing Commission has recommended a reduction in the crack-cocaine sentences. In 2002, the Sentencing Commission informed Congress that the 100-to-1 ratio was way too high and unjustified. The commission specifically recommended lowering the ratio.

Fortunately, Congress reduced the sentencing disparities between crack and powder cocaine with the Fair Sentencing Act of 2010. Yet a significant difference remains between the two, as there still is an 18-to-1 difference, meaning that the penalties for crack-cocaine offenses are nearly 20 times higher than offenses for powder cocaine.

The sentencing disparities had racial overtones.

The crack-cocaine sentencing laws in the 1980s had a severely disproportionate impact on the African-American community. In 2000, less than 6 percent of crack-cocaine drug offenders were white, while more than 80 percent were black. As a result, the war on drugs has led to racial profiling in drug cases and far too many arrests of African Americans. Criminal defense attorney John V. Elmore notes: "Drug crimes have removed more African-Americans from their homes than any other types of crimes."[6] He explains that the primary reason for the removal of many young African-American men from society to prison is the crack-cocaine sentencing laws. He notes that nearly 90 percent of defendants charged with crack-cocaine crimes are black.[7]

Gang leader Kevin F. Williams-Davis spoke for nearly 75 minutes at his sentencing hearing in a Washington, D.C., courtroom, where he received a life sentence for his alleged role in a murder related to his gang's drug trade. Williams-Davis blasted the legal system for the war on drugs. "This war on drugs is truly a war on young black men," he said. "Why is it that when young black males come into this courthouse they are made out to be mobsters or villains?"[8]

"How can you go to an inner-city family and tell them their son is given 20 years, while someone in the suburbs who's using powdered cocaine in greater quantities can get off with 90 days' probation?" asked Laura Murphy, director of the Washington, D.C., chapter of the American Civil Liberties Union (ACLU). "When people understand the truth about the way these laws are imposed . . . then I think a sleeping giant is going to roar."[9]

Data from the United States Sentencing Commission establishes that the vast majority of those sentenced under federal laws for crack-cocaine offenses are African Americans. In fact, in 2006, more than 80 percent of those sentenced were black. By contrast, the percentages for federal sentences for powder-cocaine offenses that year were 14 percent for whites and 58 percent for Hispanics. Lanny A. Breuer, an assistant U.S. attorney general for the U.S. Department of Justice, concluded, "The impact of these laws has fueled the belief across the country that federal cocaine laws are unjust."[10]

QUOTABLE

Lanny A. Breuer, assistant attorney general, Criminal Division, U.S. Department of Justice

Ensuring fairness in the criminal justice system is also critically important. Public trust and confidence are essential elements of an effective criminal justice system—our laws and their enforcement must not only be fair, but they must also be perceived as fair. The perception of unfairness undermines governmental authority in the criminal justice process. It leads victims and witnesses of crime to think twice before cooperating with law enforcement, tempts jurors to ignore the law and facts when judging a criminal case, and draws the public into questioning the motives of governmental officials.

Changing these perceptions will strengthen law enforcement through increased public trust and cooperation, coupled with the availability of legal tools that are both tough and fair. This Administration is committed to reviewing criminal justice issues to ensure that our law enforcement officers and prosecutors have the tools they need to combat crime and ensure public safety, while simultaneously working to root out any unwarranted and unintended disparities in the criminal justice process that may exist.

There is no better place to start our work than with a thorough examination of federal cocaine sentencing policy. Since the United States Sentencing Commission first reported 15 years ago on the differences in sentencing between crack and powder cocaine, a consensus has developed that the federal cocaine sentencing laws should be reassessed. Indeed, over the past 15 years, our understanding of crack and powder cocaine, their effects on the community, and the public safety imperatives surrounding all drug trafficking has evolved. That refined understanding, coupled with the need to ensure fundamental fairness in our sentencing laws, policy, and practice, necessitates a change. We think this change should be addressed in this Congress, and we look forward to working with you and other members of Congress over the coming months to address the sentencing disparity between crack and powder cocaine.

Source: Statement of Lanny A. Breuer, assistant U.S. attorney general, at the U.S Senate Judiciary Committee hearing, "Restoring Fairness to Federal Sentencing: Addressing the Crack-Powder Disparity," April 29, 2009.

A few judges even determined that the crack-to-powder-cocaine differential was so great that it violated the Equal Protection Clause of the Fourteenth Amendment, which provides that the government should treat people who are similarly situated with a degree of equality. U.S. District Court Judge Clyde S. Cahill famously found that the disparities were "so significantly disproportional that it shocks the conscience of the Court."[11] He determined that the 100-to-1 ratio was a violation

FROM THE BENCH

United States v. Clary, 846 F.Supp. 768 (E.D Mo. 1994)

Before this Court are two different sentencing provisions contained within the same statute for possession and distribution of different forms of the same drug. The difference—the key difference—is that possession and distribution of 50 grams of crack cocaine carries the same mandatory minimum sentence of 10 years imprisonment as possession and distribution of 5,000 grams of powder cocaine. Both provisions punish the same drug, but penalize crack cocaine 100 times more than powder cocaine!

Congress tells us that the rationale for this sentencing dichotomy which produces harsher punishment for involvement with crack cocaine is because it is so much more dangerous than powder cocaine. As "proof," Congress relied upon endless media accounts of crack's increased threat to society. While Congress may have had well-intentioned concerns, the Court is equally aware that this one provision, the crack statute, has been directly responsible for incarcerating nearly an entire generation of young black American men for very long periods, usually during the most productive time of their lives. Inasmuch as crack and powder cocaine are really the same drug (powder cocaine is "cooked" with baking soda for about a minute to make crack), it appears likely that race rather than conduct was the determining factor.

Although both statutory provisions purport to punish criminal activity for both crack and powder cocaine, the blacks using crack are punished with much longer sentences than whites using the same amount of powder cocaine. This disparity of equal protection and even went so far as to state: "Prosecution based on race is obviously discriminatory even if it is occasioned by *unconscious* racism."[12]

While the U.S. Court of Appeals for the Eighth Circuit later reversed Judge Cahill's decision, many people still believe that he was correct in noting the racial aspects of the sentencing law. Moreover, even many law enforcement officials recognize that the crack-powder cocaine disparities presented serious problems.

is so significantly disproportional that it shocks the conscience of the Court and invokes examination....

This Court recognizes that the control of crime is the most important goal of sentencing, and a firm and certain punishment must be the major goal in criminal justice. However, such punishment must be fair; it must fit the particulars of the offense and must acknowledge characteristics of individuals.

Let it be further understood that this Court would play no role in furthering the belief that drugs are to be condoned or ignored. Naturally, the greatest effectiveness would come from controlling those nearest the source of the drugs, but even the couriers and street peddlers facilitate the distribution of the deadly substances and they, too, must be punished but to a degree commensurate with their culpability.

The "100 to 1" ratio, coupled with mandatory minimum sentencing provided by federal statute, has created a situation that reeks with inhumanity and injustice. The scales of justice have been turned topsy turvy so that those masterminds, the "kingpins" of drug trafficking, escape detection, while those whose role is minimal, even trivial, are hoisted on the spears of an enraged electorate and at the pinnacle of their youth are imprisoned for years while those most responsible for the evil of the day remain free.

Having clearly stated the Court's conviction that crime cannot be reduced without stern and prompt punishment as well as long range plans to reduce criminal activities, the Court now feels emboldened to express a viewpoint designed to eliminate the disproportional punishment for crack, which would enhance the credibility of the government among black citizens and help restore their faith in believing that equal justice is for all.

The disparities cause disrespect for the criminal justice system.

While crack did have a serious impact on the criminal justice system, the impact has always been exaggerated. The United States Sentencing Commission bluntly stated that "the epidemic of crack cocaine use by youth never materialized to the extent feared."[13] In reality, most crack users were already hard-core drug addicts. Despite the rise in crack use, as time has passed, the crime rate associated with crack has declined and murder rates have gone down.[14]

Perhaps the most damaging aspect of the severe crack-powder cocaine sentencing disparities is the impact on many

QUOTABLE

John F. Timoney, chief of police, Miami Police Department

Others have testified today on the genesis of the 100 to 1 disparity and on the efforts of many, including the United States Sentencing Commission, to try to rectify or mitigate the disparity. To date none of these efforts have been effective, having, for whatever reason, fallen on deaf ears. I am here today to lend my voice to the chorus pleading with the Congress to right a wrong. . . .

Making an artificial distinction about a particular form of the same drug is a distinction without a difference and that's bad enough. But when the distinction results in a dramatic disparity in sentencing along racial lines, then that distinction is simply un-American and intolerable. Furthermore, it defies logic from a law enforcement perspective.

Here's what I mean: If I arrest a guy carrying five grams of crack—that's less than a fifth of an ounce—I figure this is a low-level street corner drug dealer. Or maybe he's someone carrying a lot [of] crack for his own personal consumption. But if I arrest a guy with 500 grams of powder cocaine—that's more than a pound—I figure this guy is a serious trafficker. The notion that both of these guys are equal and deserve the same time in jail is ludicrous.

Now let me take my two guys and show you the monetary value of their illegal contraband. In Miami today you can purchase five grams of crack for around everyday people. The disparities cause many people to question the underlying fairness of the criminal justice system. When many people in society question the fairness of the criminal justice system, there are major problems, most notably, rebellion against the system. Law professor and author Paul Butler, a former federal prosecutor, has gone so far as to suggest that African-American defendants should try to convince juries to refuse to convict under an unjust law, a phenomenon known as jury nullification.[15]

Because the crack-to-powder-cocaine disparities in sentencing are so high, it causes some to believe that the government is behind the crack epidemic. Another systemic problem is that it

$150. If it is in Philadelphia or New York, my two prior cities, you may pay a higher cost of around $200. In Miami, my undercover officers are paying anywhere from $700 to $1,000 per ounce for powder cocaine and around $14,000 for a half-kilo, 500 grams. In Philadelphia or New York you may pay a little more. Bottom line is there is a hell of a difference between $150 and $14,000. If you were to present these numbers to the average 8th grader and ask them which was the narcotic trafficker, they would have little problem with the answer. It's that simple.

Finally, when unfair laws are passed, police officers see the impact at the local level. Citizens do notice these things, and they become cynical. I remember back in 1974 when President Ford issued a pardon to former President Nixon. I was a young cop patrolling the streets of the South Bronx, and I was amazed at how people would throw it back in our face if we made an arrest; they'd say, "Oh, Nixon gets pardoned; only poor people get arrested."

Of course a lot of that was just street-level nonsense, but the point is that police departments face a much more difficult challenge gaining the trust of their communities if there are glaring inequities in the justice system that are allowed to persist. These inequities breed cynicism and mistrust and should be eliminated.

Source: Testimony of John F. Timoney, chief of police, Miami Police Department, before the Subcommittee on Crime and Drugs, U.S. Senate Judiciary Committee on "Restoring Fairness to Federal Sentencing: Addressing the Crack-Powder Disparity," April 29, 2009.

simply makes people question whether they should support the criminal justice system in general. Law professor Michael O'Hear explains:

> A growing body of social psychology research links citizen perceptions of biased and disrespectful treatment by legal authorities to citizen disrespect of the law and legal system, and ultimately to reduced motivation to obey the law and cooperate with the authorities.[16]

The Fair Sentencing Act should be applied retroactively.

In 2010, Congress made a positive first step in passing the Fair Sentencing Act, which reduces the crack-to-powder-cocaine sentencing disparities. There is, however, still much work to be done. Many inmates still languish in jail for nonviolent crack-cocaine drug offenses because they were sentenced under the old, unfair guidelines. "But the people who personified the injustice will continue to suffer," said Jennifer Seltzer Stitt, director of federal legislative affairs for Families Against Mandatory Minimums, a group that opposes the harsh sentencing guidelines. "A really good analogy that someone else used is when a car company discovers something is broken, they fix it and then they recall all the cars and fix them."[17]

Summary

The 100-to-1 ratio for crack-cocaine and powder-cocaine offenses was unfair, racially discriminatory, and bad public policy, but the current 18-to-1 ratio is hardly any better. A low-level street dealer in crack cocaine should not receive the same sentence as a high-level drug kingpin who is caught with large amounts of powder cocaine.

The crack-cocaine sentencing guidelines have had a terribly disproportionate racial impact on black Americans. The vast majority of those convicted and then sentenced under the Anti-

Drug Abuse Act of 1986 were African-American defendants. This led to a breakdown in family structure for many African-American families. Furthermore, the sentencing disparities have created systemic problems for law enforcement officials, who must deal with many people who believe that the criminal justice system is unfair and targets those in their communities.

Crack Cocaine Offenses Should Be Punished at a Higher Rate

When *New Jack City* hit movie screens across the country in 1991, it had a profound impact on its audiences. The film told the sordid fictional story of drug kingpin Nino Brown, portrayed by actor Wesley Snipes, lording over New York City's crack-cocaine empire with his gang, Cash Money Brothers. It showed the devastation that the Brown drug crew created in New York's poor neighborhoods. It showed the lives of those who became lost to crack addiction. It depicted women selling their bodies for the next hit of crack cocaine.

While *New Jack City* was a fictional movie with some exaggerations, it was based on hard-core realities that existed in too many poor, urban neighborhoods. The crack trade overwhelmed many neighborhoods in a way no other illegal drug had ever done before.

Crack cocaine is different than powder cocaine.

Unlike powder cocaine, crack cocaine can be sold in smaller quantities and can be accessed by many more people. The U.S. Supreme Court explained that "smoking crack cocaine allows the body to absorb the drug much faster than inhaling powder cocaine, and thus produces a shorter, more intense high."[1] Professor Randall Kennedy explains in his incisive book *Race, Crime, and the Law*: "Even if crack and powder were otherwise identical, the greater marketability of crack means that it has more potential reach than powder and can thus be reasonably perceived as more of a social danger."[2]

"Crack clearly causes more trouble than powdered cocaine," Dr. Robert Byck, a Yale medical school professor, told the *New York Times*. "When rock was introduced, the number of hospitalizations for cocaine impairment went way up, and the number of people addicted went way up."[3]

"Crack cocaine changed the drug abuse landscape," Wayne J. Roques of the Drug Enforcement Administration (DEA) remarked to the *New York Times*.

> The rapid onset of addiction, its propensity to cause hyperactive violence, destroy the cardiovascular health of the user, and damage drug-exposed fetuses, has propelled us in an ever-quickening downward spiral. This epidemic also gives the lie to the theory that cheap prices for drugs would result in a reduction in crime.[4]

Congress created the sentencing disparity for many, nonracial reasons.

Congress had many reasons for determining that greater sentences should be imposed on those who dealt in crack cocaine as opposed to powder cocaine. These included: 1) crack was more addictive; 2) crack users and sellers were more violent; 3)

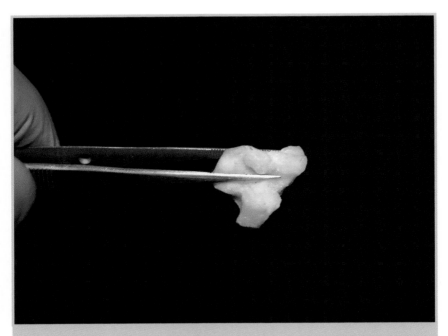

Here, a lab worker tests a sample of crack cocaine to determine quality. Crack cocaine—also called base, cavvy, rock, hard, iron, or just crack—is the freebase form of cocaine that can be smoked. Between roughly 1984 and 1990, the United States experienced a "crack epidemic," which refers to the surge of crack houses and crack-cocaine use in major cities across America during that time.

crack was more harmful to users than powder cocaine; 4) crack was more predominantly used by younger people than powder cocaine; and 5) crack was more potent and its lower cost made it more popular.[5]

Federal appeals courts have rejected the argument that the crack-cocaine sentencing guidelines violate the Equal Protection Clause. For example, the U.S. Court of Appeals for the Eighth Circuit, in its opinion in *United States v. Clary*, reversed an oft-

FROM THE BENCH

United States v. Clary, 34 F.3d 709 (8th Cir. 1994)

The district court's painstakingly-crafted opinion demonstrates the careful consideration it gave not only to the testimony before it, but also to the voluminous documents introduced by Clary, including both law review and text materials. This case undoubtedly presents the most complete record on this issue to come before this court. Nevertheless, we are satisfied that both the record before the district court and the district court's findings fall short of establishing that Congress acted with a discriminatory purpose in enacting the statute, and that Congress selected or reaffirmed a particular course of action "at least in part 'because of,' not merely 'in spite of' its adverse effects upon an identifiable group. . . ."

We also question the court's reliance on media-created stereotypes of crack dealers and its conclusion that this information "undoubtedly served as the touchstone that influenced racial perceptions held by legislators and the public as related to the 'crack epidemic.'" Although the placement of newspaper and magazine articles in the *Congressional Record* indicates that this information may have affected at least some legislators, these articles hardly demonstrate that the stereotypical images "undoubtedly" influenced the legislators' racial perceptions. It is too long a leap from newspaper and magazine articles to an inference that Congress enacted the crack statute because of its adverse effect on African American males, instead of the stated purpose of responding to the serious impact of a rapidly-developing and particularly-dangerous form of drug use. Similarly, the evidence of the haste with which Congress acted and the action it took is as easily explained by the seriousness of the perceived problem as by racial animus.

The district court's final conclusion that objective evidence supports the belief that racial animus was a motivating factor in enacting the crack statute further belies the weakness of its position. . . .

Similarly, David Courtwright, who described himself as an historian of drug laws, stated that he did not know if racial considerations led to the passage of the crack laws, and that he had no special or expert knowledge as to the motives of the legislators voting for the 1986 law.

For the most part, the other witnesses that testified before the district court were medical witnesses, several of whom contested the medical information before the Senate that showed differences between crack and powder cocaine. Scientific disagreement with testimony in congressional hearings, offered at a later time and after additional research, simply does not establish discriminatory purpose, or for that matter, a lack of scientific support for Congress' action.

cited federal district court opinion that had found the guidelines to be racially discriminatory.[6] The appeals court determined that media reports and "unconscious racism" were simply not enough to show that Congress acted with a discriminatory purpose.

Crack cocaine leads to violence.

Users of crack cocaine are more likely than users of powder cocaine to be violent. Why is this the case? Much of it can be traced to the difference in the drug's addictiveness. Surveys indicate that users of crack cocaine frequently resort to violence to acquire money to feed their drug habit. Researchers said that users of crack cocaine commit more violent acts because freebasing crack cocaine delivers more dosage of the drug directly to the brain.[7]

A 1988 survey, done when the crack epidemic was destroying communities of drug users, indicated that 31 percent said "uncontrollable violence" was one side effect of the drug upon them. Another 17 percent said that they carried a firearm, and 13 percent said that they committed armed robbery to obtain money to buy more crack.[8]

William Bennett, the nation's drug czar in the late 1980s, did not exaggerate when he said: "Far too many of the city's streets and neighborhoods now belong not to their good and decent residents, but to criminals who subvert public order and public health."[9]

"What about the gangs, the rivalries, the shootings, the killings?" asked Jim Shedd, a DEA agent who is involved in the fight against crack cocaine. "Everybody's forgotten about the amount of violence that goes with crack cocaine. It's not a racist thing, but unfortunately that's what it's turned into."[10]

Still today, those who traffic in crack cocaine terrify law-abiding citizens and commit an unreal amount of violence. R. Alexander Acosta, U.S. attorney for the Southern District of Florida, explained this in a public hearing of the United States Sentencing Commission in 2006:

Cocaine base is more closely associated with street-level gang violence than other drugs, including cocaine powder. There's substantial proof that the violent gangs are deeply involved in trafficking in cocaine base especially in metropolitan areas and certain neighborhoods. There's also substantial proof that cocaine base is associated with violence to a greater degree than other controlled substances, including cocaine powder. In short, the violent drug gangs that plague our cities are populated by members who peddle cocaine base and use guns and use violence to promote their drug trafficking activities.[11]

QUOTABLE

Legal commentator Elizabeth Tison

The most lethal danger facing minorities in their day-to-day lives is not white, racist officials of the state, but private, violent criminals who attack those most vulnerable to them without regard to racial identity. The flip side of racially invidious over-enforcement of the criminal law is often minimized. Racially invidious under-enforcement purposefully denies minority victims of violence the things that all persons legitimately expect from the state: civil order and, in the event crimes are committed, best efforts to apprehend and punish offenders. If dealers in crack cocaine have their liberty significantly restricted, this will afford greater liberties to the majority of citizens who are the potential victims of drug dealing and accompanying violent behavior. When the sentencing provisions are condemned as unfair to a defendant sentenced under crack statutes, that same defendant has been duly convicted of dealing in crack cocaine. It is important to keep in mind that for nearly every defendant sentenced under harsh crack provisions, there are numerous children on the streets to whom that dealer will never have the opportunity to sell crack cocaine.

Source: Elizabeth Tison, "Amending the Sentencing Guidelines for Cocaine Offenses: The 100-to-1 Ratio Is Not as 'Cracked' Up As Some Suggest," 27 *Southern Illinois University Law Journal* 413, 434 (2003).

Racism did not inspire the crack-cocaine sentencing laws.

Critics charge that racism alone motivated the federal drug laws in the 1980s that provided greater sentences for crack-cocaine

Testimony of Deputy U.S. Attorney General Larry Thompson on Crack Cocaine Federal Sentencing

We understand that the Commission is considering lowering penalties for crack offenders. After thorough study and internal debate, we have concluded that the current federal policy and guidelines for sentencing crack cocaine offenses are proper. It would therefore be more appropriate to address the differential between crack and powder cocaine by recommending that penalties for powder cocaine be increased.

Current research shows that crack is an extremely dangerous substance for many reasons. The most common routes of administration for crack and powder cause crack to be the more psychologically addictive of the substances. This makes crack cocaine more dangerous, resulting in far more emergency-room episodes and public-facility treatment admissions than powder cocaine, despite the fact that powder cocaine is much more widely used.

Further, crack can easily be broken down and packaged into small and inexpensive quantities for distribution . . . making it particularly attractive to some of the more vulnerable members of our society. . . .

Additionally, the open-air street markets and crack houses used for the distribution of crack cocaine contribute heavily to the deterioration of neighborhoods and communities. . . .

The present crack market is associated with violent crime to a greater extent than that of cocaine powder. Crack offenders are more frequently associated with weapons use than powder cocaine offenders. For example, in FY [fiscal year] 2000, weapons were involved in 10.6% of federal powder convictions, and 21.3% of federal crack convictions. Federal crack offenses are also more frequently associated with violence and bodily injury than powder cocaine offenses. Although the Commission has proposed separate enhancements for offenders who employ weapons, violence by offenders themselves is only a portion of the crime that crack causes and thus would not reflect the dangers of the drug.

offenses. Yet racism did not motivate these laws. These laws were drafted because of an epidemic of violence that all but destroyed many urban black communities. The laws were passed to provide protection to the people who lived in those communities.

Crack is linked to robbery and assault by customers seeking to finance their habits. Crack is strongly linked to prostitution, as well. In one recent study, 86.7% of women surveyed were not involved in prostitution in the year before starting crack use; fully one-third became involved in prostitution in the year after they began use. Women who were already involved in prostitution dramatically increased their involvement, with rates nearly four times higher than before beginning crack use. And because of the incidence of prostitution among crack users to finance their habit, crack cocaine smokers have been found to have rates of HIV infection as high as those among IV drug users.

Another recent study found that women who used crack cocaine had "much higher than average rates of victimization" than women who did not. Among an Ohio sample of 171 adult female crack users, 62% had been physically attacked since the onset of crack use. Rape was reported by 32% of the women since they began using crack, and among these, 83% reported being high on crack when the rape occurred, as were an estimated 57% of the perpetrators.

These and many other statistics and studies tell the story of the devastation that cocaine, and crack cocaine specifically, bring to the nation—especially its minority communities. Lowering crack penalties would simply send the wrong message—that we care more about crack dealers then we do about the people and the communities victimized by crack. That is something that we simply cannot support.

Further, lowering crack penalties is inconsistent with a rejuvenated national fight against illegal drug use. As we indicate in the national drug strategy, effective drug control policy, reduced to its barest essentials, has just two elements: modifying individual behavior to discourage and reduce drug use and addiction, and disrupting the market for illegal drugs. We think lowering crack penalties fails on both counts.

Source: Larry D. Thompson, deputy U.S. attorney general, testimony before the United States Sentencing Commission, March 19, 2002. http://www.justice.gov/archive/dag/testimony/2002/031902testimonyussentcomm.htm.

In his book *Race, Crime, and the Law,* professor Randall Kennedy points out that 11 of 21 African-American members of the U.S. House of Representatives then in Congress voted in favor of the greater punishment for crack-cocaine offenses. Kennedy explains that "in light of charges that the crack-powder distinction was enacted partly because of conscious or unconscious racism, it is noteworthy that *none* of the black members of Congress made that claim at the time the bill was initially discussed."[12]

Deputy U.S. Attorney General Larry Thompson explained to the United States Sentencing Commission in 2002:

> There are significant differences in the predominant manner the two substances are ingested and marketed. Based on those differences and the resulting harms to society, we believe that crack cocaine is an especially dangerous drug, and its traffickers should be subject to significantly higher penalties than traffickers of like amounts of powder.[13]

Crime victims of crack-induced violence should be remembered.

The debate about the severity of criminal sentences focuses on the rights of those trafficking in illegal drugs. Many drug traffickers commit other crimes in the pursuit and maintenance of the illegal drug trade. These drug dealers, pushers, and runners harm untold numbers of other members of the community who have to live in a daily environment of crime, fear, and intimidation. The legal system should focus more on the rights of crime victims, rather than drug dealers. Philip Coltoff, executive director of the Children's Aid Society, expressed this belief well in the *New York Times* when he explained:

> Ending prohibition would free court calendars and prison beds. But would it reduce the number of crack-

addicted babies or family violence? Crime in the streets might go down with legalization. We shouldn't confuse that with protection for the thousands of children who will still be the victims of drug users within their families, or whose own prospects spiral downward with addiction.[14]

Representative Bill McCollum of Florida made this point in Congress: "No one should forget that crack traffickers deal in death, and that they do so to the most vulnerable among us, the residents of our inner cities."[15]

Summary

There are valid reasons for imposing greater sentences for crack-cocaine offenses than for powder-cocaine crimes—and none of them have anything to do with racial bias. The sentencing guidelines for crack offenses were not passed with a racially discriminatory purpose and do not violate the Equal Protection Clause. When drawing up the penalties, Congress legitimately believed that crack cocaine was a grave problem facing the country, particularly poor urban neighborhoods.

This is not just a belief, but a fact. The reality is that crack offenses are more often associated with violence. Crack is often more addictive, leading those addicted to become desperate and violent. Crack has had a devastating impact on urban communities. Congress—rightfully concerned with crime victims when it passed this statute—should continue to maintain some distinction between crack- and powder-cocaine offenses.

Marijuana Should Be Legalized

I n 1999, John Hardin testified before a government panel about the impact of marijuana on his life—and it was not the negative kind you might imagine. He told the panel about the devastating disease hepatitis C, which had wreaked havoc over his body. "I lost 95 pounds [43 kilograms]," he said. "I tried everything; 35 different pills. Finally, doctors told me to go to Europe and try marijuana."[1] He did just that and it began to alleviate much of the excruciating pain.

Dr. George Wagoner testified a decade later in Minnesota, as the state legislature debated the merits of a medical marijuana bill. He described how marijuana relieved his wife, who was suffering great pain from ovarian cancer. "Eating lunch isn't a big deal until you can't. . . . The relief was as complete and dramatic as any I've experienced in my practice."[2] Similarly, Kathy Rippentrop testified that marijuana alleviated much suffering for her mother, who experienced debilitating pain from cancer. "Two puffs, two minutes, and the violent sickness was totally gone," she said. "An hour later, Mom was able to have a good meal. The stomach problems from the chemo were totally gone. It also helped her regain a quality of life that allowed her to continue to fight."[3]

Daniel J. Kane, an attorney who suffers from HIV, declared in court that marijuana provided the only relief from pain that his doctors could find. Without marijuana, the pain and nausea were unbearable. There are countless other testimonies of individuals whose lives have been helped by marijuana. Moreover, legal marijuana use for medicinal purposes has widespread support. Conservative writer William F. Buckley Jr. once wrote: "The government should treat marijuana more or less the same way it treats alcohol: It should regulate it, control it, tax it, and make it illegal only for children."[4]

Marijuana has definite medical benefits.

In the early 1960s, the editors of a British medical magazine called for the legalization of marijuana, arguing that the drug's effects are no worse than those of alcohol.[5] In the 1990s, more American scholars began to call for a fundamental change in how marijuana was viewed. Dr. Lester Grinspoon, an associate professor of psychiatry at Harvard Medical School, coauthored a book in 1993 titled *Marijuana: The Forbidden Medicine.* He told a reporter for the *Washington Post* that, as a medicine, marijuana had definite benefits for treating severe nausea, multiple sclerosis, migraine headaches, and other ailments. He noted:

> It relieves the symptoms—muscle spasms, tremors—of multiple sclerosis. It is an analgesic for chronic pain and relieves migraines and menstrual pain. Marijuana is an important medicine we have been overlooking or dismissing. I think it will prove to be one of the least toxic drugs in the pharmacopoeia.[6]

A study commissioned by the U.S. government in 1999 found that marijuana had some medical benefits. Eleven experts at the Institute of Medicine determined that marijuana had some positive benefits for patients experiencing nausea, weight

QUOTABLE

Daniel J. Kane

I have been HIV-infected for at least 12 years and severely ill for the past four. Over the past year, my health has improved as my doctor and I have adjusted, readjusted and, in some cases, changed altogether my treatment plan. The information he has provided, and his willingness to constantly reassess my condition and seek more effective treatments, have guided me through many painful and demoralizing periods. He has been candid with me about the risks of the medications I have taken, and he has been extremely cautious about prescribing medications for pain or for anxiety. He has done everything possible to reduce adverse side effects that were often intolerable. When I developed wasting syndrome, he tried everything possible to help me regain my weight and restore my energy.

The process was often very painful. My doctor tried to relieve my nausea by prescribing a series of anti-nausea medications, including Compazine and Phenergan, but those drugs were in pill form and I couldn't bear to swallow them. . . . The only reason I agreed to these miserable, and ultimately useless, treatments was because I trusted my doctor. I knew that he was doing everything possible to give me relief and keep me alive.

In August of 1996, . . . my doctor informed me that marijuana, in small quantities, might act as both an anti-nauseant and an appetite stimulant. I tried smoking marijuana to combat the nausea. I found that it reduced my nausea and restored my appetite, allowing me to eat and regain my strength with no noticeable side effects. Having tried the other medications, I know from personal experience that, at least for me, nothing compares to marijuana in terms of results. I use marijuana only a few times a week—sometimes less—but since I started, I have been able to eat and I've regained weight, muscle mass and hope. That small amount of marijuana has enabled me to function in the world again.

Source: Declarations of Daniel J. Kane in *Conant v. McCaffrey*. http://www.drugpolicy.org/marijuana/medical/challenges/cases/conant/declarations/kane.cfm.

According to the United Nations, marijuana is the most commonly used illicit drug in the world. A plant indigenous to Central and South Asia, it is now grown worldwide, including in the United States. Archaeologists have discovered evidence of the inhalation of cannabis smoke by human beings going as far back as the third millennium B.C.

loss associated with HIV/AIDS, and/or various pains. The study recommended that marijuana be given under close monitoring to those patients who did not respond well to other therapies.[7]

Viewed from hindsight, these early studies appear quite prescient, as scientists and doctors have since documented definite benefits from the medicinal use of marijuana. The National Organization for the Reform of Marijuana Laws (NORML) has identified 19 diseases marijuana is helpful in treating. They are:

Alzheimer's disease, amyotrophic lateral sclerosis, chronic pain, diabetes mellitus, dystonia, fibromyalgia, gastrointestinal disorders, gliomas, hepatitis C, human immunodeficiency virus, hypertension, incontinence, methicillin-resistant *staphylloccus aureus,* multiple sclerosis,

THE LETTER OF THE LAW

The following are excerpts from state laws regulating medical marijuana:

California's Compassionate Use Act
§ 11362.5. Use of marijuana for medical purposes

 (a) This section shall be known and may be cited as the Compassionate Use Act of 1996.

 (b) (1) The people of the State of California hereby find and declare that the purposes of the Compassionate Use Act of 1996 are as follows:

  (A) To ensure that seriously ill Californians have the right to obtain and use marijuana for medical purposes where the medical use is deemed appropriate and has been recommended by a physician who has determined that the person's health would benefit from the use of marijuana in the treatment of cancer, anorexia, AIDS, chronic pain, spasticity, glaucoma, arthritis, migraine, or any other illness for which marijuana provides relief.

  (B) To ensure that patients and their primary caregivers who obtain and use marijuana for medical purposes upon the recommendation of a physician are not subject to criminal prosecution or sanction.

  (C) To encourage the federal and state governments to implement a plan to provide for the safe and affordable distribution of marijuana to all patients in medical need of marijuana.

 (2) Nothing in this Act shall be construed to supersede legislation prohibiting persons from engaging in conduct that endangers others, nor to condone the diversion of marijuana for nonmedical purposes.

 (c) Notwithstanding any other provision of law, no physician in this state shall be punished, or denied any right or privilege, for having recommended marijuana to a patient for medical purposes.

osteoporosis, pruritus, rheumatoid arthritis, sleep apnea, and Tourette's syndrome.[8]

Owing to marijuana's clear benefits, more and more jurisdictions have gradually moved toward allowing medicinal use of

(d) Section 11357, relating to the possession of marijuana, and Section 11358, relating to the cultivation of marijuana, shall not apply to a patient, or to a patient's primary caregiver, who possesses or cultivates marijuana for the personal medical purposes of the patient upon the written or oral recommendation or approval of a physician.

(e) For the purposes of this section, "primary caregiver" means the individual designated by the person exempted under this act who has consistently assumed responsibility for the housing, health, or safety of that person.*

Virginia Law on Medical Marijuana

§ 18.2-251.1. Possession or distribution of marijuana for medical purposes permitted.

A. No person shall be prosecuted under § 18.2-250 or § 18.2-250.1 for the possession of marijuana or tetrahydrocannabinol when that possession occurs pursuant to a valid prescription issued by a medical doctor in the course of his professional practice for treatment of cancer or glaucoma.

B. No medical doctor shall be prosecuted under § 18.2-248 or § 18.2-248.1 for dispensing or distributing marijuana or tetrahydrocannabinol for medical purposes when such action occurs in the course of his professional practice for treatment of cancer or glaucoma.

C. No pharmacist shall be prosecuted under §§ 18.2-248 to 18.2-248.1 for dispensing or distributing marijuana or tetrahydrocannabinol to any person who holds a valid prescription of a medical doctor for such substance issued in the course of such doctor's professional practice for treatment of cancer or glaucoma.**

*Cal Health & Safety Code § 11362.5
**Va. Code Ann. § 18.2-251.1 (2010)

marijuana. In May 2010, for example, the District of Columbia Council unanimously agreed to legalize medicinal marijuana and establish some sort of regulatory framework for cultivating the drug and regulating prescriptions.[9] Across the country, 15 states have approved the use of medical marijuana for people with chronic or debilitating diseases.

Efforts are even under way in the U.S. Congress to provide some relief to those who could benefit from marijuana from a medical standpoint. In June 2009, Representative Barney Frank

Drug Policy Alliance on Marijuana Being Addictive

Myth: Marijuana is a Gateway Drug. Even if marijuana itself causes minimal harm, it is a dangerous substance because it leads to the use of "harder drugs" like heroin, LSD, and cocaine.

Fact: Marijuana does not cause people to use hard drugs. What the gateway theory presents as a causal explanation is a statistic association between common and uncommon drugs, an association that changes over time as different drugs increase and decrease in prevalence. Marijuana is the most popular illegal drug in the United States today. Therefore, people who have used less popular drugs such as heroin, cocaine, and LSD, are likely to have also used marijuana. Most marijuana users never use any other illegal drug. Indeed, for the large majority of people, marijuana is a terminus rather than a gateway drug.

Myth: Marijuana is Highly Addictive. Long-term marijuana users experience physical dependence and withdrawal, and often need professional drug treatment to break their marijuana habits.

Fact: Most people who smoke marijuana smoke it only occasionally. A small minority of Americans—less than 1 percent—smoke marijuana on a daily basis. An even smaller minority develop a dependence on marijuana. Some people who smoke marijuana heavily and frequently stop without difficulty. Others seek help from drug treatment professionals. Marijuana does not cause physical dependence. If people experience withdrawal symptoms at all, they are remarkably mild.

of Massachusetts introduced the Medical Marijuana Patient Protection Act.[10]

Marijuana is not a gateway drug.

While medical benefits may be the strongest argument for legalizing at least some forms of marijuana, it is by far the only argument. Much of the rhetoric against marijuana in the war on drugs has been wrong. For years, the antidrug movement has claimed that marijuana is a gateway drug, that people

---

Myth: Marijuana's Harms Have Been Proved Scientifically. In the 1960s and 1970s, many people believed that marijuana was harmless. Today we know that marijuana is much more dangerous than previously believed.

Fact: In 1972, after reviewing the scientific evidence, the National Commission on Marihuana and Drug Abuse concluded that while marijuana was not entirely safe, its dangers had been grossly overstated. Since then, researchers have conducted thousands of studies of humans, animals, and cell cultures. None reveal any findings dramatically different from those described by the National Commission in 1972. In 1995, based on thirty years of scientific research, editors of the British medical journal *Lancet* concluded that "the smoking of cannabis, even long term, is not harmful to health."

Myth: Marijuana Causes Crime. Marijuana users commit more property offenses than nonusers. Under the influence of marijuana, people become irrational, aggressive, and violent.

Fact: Every serious scholar and government commission examining the relationship between marijuana use and crime has reached the same conclusion: marijuana does not cause crime. The vast majority of marijuana users do not commit crimes other than the crime of possessing marijuana. Among marijuana users who do commit crimes, marijuana plays no causal role. Almost all human and animal studies show that marijuana decreases rather than increases aggression.

Source: Drug Policy Alliance, "Myths and Facts about Marijuana." http://www.drugpolicy.org/marijuana/factsmyths/#gateway; http://www.drugpolicy.org/marijuana/factsmyths/#addictive; http://www.drugpolicy.org/marijuana/factsmyths/#harms; http://www.drugpolicy.org/marijuana/factsmyths/#crime.

who smoke a few marijuana cigarettes have a strong chance of becoming hard-core drug addicts. The reality, however, is much different. A 2010 study conducted at the University of New Hampshire found clearly that marijuana was not a gateway drug. "While marijuana use may serve as a gateway to other illicit drug use in adolescence, our results indicate that the effect may be short-lived, subsiding by age 21," the study's researchers said.[11] "In light of these findings, we urge U.S. drug control policymakers to consider stress and life-course approaches in their pursuit of solutions to the 'drug problem,'" said Dr. Karen Van Gundy, one of the study's authors.[12]

Taxing marijuana could raise money and help fight more harmful drugs.

Marijuana should be treated the same way as alcohol and tobacco—that is, regulated, taxed, and controlled by the

---

QUOTABLE

NORML

By any objective standard, marijuana prohibition is an abject failure.

Nationwide, U.S. law enforcement have arrested over 20 million American citizens for marijuana offenses since 1965, yet today marijuana is more prevalent than ever before, adolescents have easier access to marijuana than ever before, the drug is on average more potent than ever before, and there is more violence associated with the illegal marijuana trade than ever before.

Over 100 million Americans nationally have used marijuana despite prohibition, and one in ten—according to current government survey data—use it regularly. The criminal prohibition of marijuana has not dissuaded anyone from using marijuana or reduced its availability; however, the strict enforcement of this policy has adversely impacted the lives and careers of millions of people who simply elected to use a substance to relax that is objectively safer than alcohol.

Source: NORML (National Organization for the Reform of Marijuana Laws). http://norml. org/index.cfm?Group_ID=8110.

government. These products are legalized for adults and criminalized for children. Just as adults can purchase alcohol and cigarettes, they should be able to purchase marijuana, and children should be denied access, just as children are denied access to alcohol and cigarettes.

Instead, taxes could be placed on marijuana and the money derived from these taxes could be used to battle crime caused by those using much harder illegal drugs, such as cocaine or heroin or methamphetamines.

Summary

Marijuana should be legalized and treated the same as alcohol and tobacco. It should be legalized for adults and prohibited for children. Those who sell marijuana to children should be punished, but the government should not continue with a failed total prohibition policy that does not have the support of a large segment of the population. Moreover, marijuana has serious positive medical benefits. That is why several states have laws on the books that allow for the medicinal use of marijuana.

Legalization would help to dispel many myths about the use of marijuana. It is not a gateway drug to other more powerful illegal drugs. It does not cause people to overdose and die. It does not make people aggressive and/or cause them to commit violent crimes. As a proven medicinal substance with few side effects, marijuana should be an option for adults living in a free society.

Marijuana Is a Harmful, Illegal, and Addictive Drug

A middle-aged man gave his testimony on how his life had spiraled out of control. He had lost his wife, children, and job. He had lost all sense of self-worth and self-respect. He had borrowed money from friends and never repaid them. He even stole from his wife, children, mother, and other family members. He did whatever he could to feed his growing drug addiction. The thing he cared most about was getting high. He could not think about anything else but feeding the beast of drug addiction. His drug of choice was heroin.

When asked how he began to use heroin, he said that he had tried marijuana with an older friend when he was young. The casual use of marijuana grew into regular use of the drug when he got older. He continued his marijuana use until he graduated into more serious drugs. He thought that he had the habit under control. Soon, though, he learned that his drug habit controlled him.

Another man in his twenties talked about his addiction to methamphetamines, a growing problem in the country. His meth addiction caused him to commit various violent felonies to obtain enough money to buy more meth. He had to rob to get money. When asked how he began his downward spiral into drugs, the young man said that an older relative had let him smoke marijuana when he was 12 years old. His casual marijuana use soon developed into regular marijuana use. Thereafter began to experiment with more powerful drugs, including cocaine and LSD. He then turned to meth—an addiction he could not shake until he had become a regular visitor to the criminal justice facilities in his county.

The striking similarity between these two individuals was the beginning of their drug use: occasional recreational use of marijuana. For these two men, marijuana truly was a "gateway" drug. It is a gateway drug because it opens the door, or gate, to further drug experimentation—often with disastrous results.

Marijuana is a harmful drug.

Marijuana causes the loss of brain functioning and leads to disorientation and disillusionment. A popular movie featuring scenes with adolescent marijuana users is *Dazed and Confused*. While intended as a comedy, the movie title has an element of sad reality. When people smoke marijuana, they lose their ability to function and think as clearly as they did previously. As their cognitive powers decrease, they find they cannot operate a motor vehicle as effectively. The drug has physical side effects as well. A former Drug Enforcement Administration official said it bluntly: "Marijuana causes damaged brain cells and respiratory systems, decreased hormone production in both sexes, acute memory loss, lower immune systems, miscarriages and stillbirth."[1]

Marijuana also serves as a gateway to other more serious drugs. Countless drug addicts have admitted that their sordid journey into devastating drug addiction began when they smoked marijuana and then progressed into harder, more

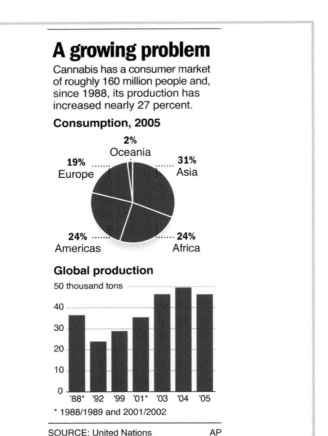

A growing problem

Cannabis has a consumer market of roughly 160 million people and, since 1988, its production has increased nearly 27 percent.

Consumption, 2005

- 2% Oceania
- 31% Asia
- 19% Europe
- 24% Americas
- 24% Africa

Global production

50 thousand tons

'88* '92 '99 '01* '03 '04 '05

* 1988/1989 and 2001/2002

SOURCE: United Nations   AP

This graphic shows global production and consumption of marijuana between 1988 and 2005. In virtually every part of the world, marijuana use increased during that period, despite prohibitions against it.

dangerous drugs. "Marijuana is frequently mentioned by drug-control specialists as being a stepping stone or gateway to drugs such as crack cocaine and heroin," Bernard Gavzer writes. "This is essentially based on admissions by cocaine and heroin users that they used marijuana before getting on hard drugs."[2]

Studies have confirmed that those individuals who smoke marijuana at an early age are far more likely to develop serious drug problems later in life. Those who abuse heroin and cocaine usually began their drug habits by smoking marijuana. These studies show that "the more puffs of marijuana you take, the more likely you move on to injections and snorting of even more dangerous drugs."[3]

Perhaps the most harmful aspect of marijuana is that it truly serves as a gateway to other harder and more dangerous

QUOTABLE

Jim McDonough, director, Florida Office of Drug Control

- There is a strong correlation between marijuana and other drug abuse, with marijuana almost always occurring first.

- Marijuana, all by itself, is a dangerous drug.

- There is a strong correlation between marijuana use and schizophrenia.

- Marijuana itself is addictive.

- Youth marijuana use correlates highly with violence, truancy, and other behavioral problems.

- The younger the marijuana user, the more psychological and physiological damage done, and the more likely that other drugs will follow.

- Smoking three marijuana joints a day can cause the equivalent respiratory damage associated with 20 cigarettes a day. Marijuana smokers show significantly more respiratory symptoms than people who don't smoke it.

- Prolonged use can cause attention deficit and deterioration in memory.

Source: Jim McDonough, "Wrong Lesson from Marijuana Gateway Study," *The Record*, December 17, 2002.

drugs. The pro-legalization side often dismisses the "gateway" argument out of hand, but many experts have confirmed the phenomenon. A police officer explained it: "A gateway drug is just that. It opens the door to using other drugs. You've broken a barrier, so it's easier to move on to something else."[4] A school superintendent echoed similar thoughts after years of working in the school system: "The thing that worries me

U.S. Drug Enforcement Administration

Q: Does marijuana pose health risks to users?

- Marijuana is an addictive drug with significant health consequences to its users and others. Many harmful short-term and long-term problems have been documented with its use:

- The short-term effects of marijuana use include: memory loss, distorted perception, trouble with thinking and problem solving, loss of motor skills, decrease in muscle strength, increased heart rate, and anxiety.

- In recent years there has been a dramatic increase in the number of emergency room mentions of marijuana use. From 1993–2000, the number of emergency room marijuana mentions more than tripled.

- There are also many long-term health consequences of marijuana use. According to the National Institutes of Health, studies show that someone who smokes five joints per week may be taking in as many cancer-causing chemicals as someone who smokes a full pack of cigarettes every day.

- Marijuana contains more than 400 chemicals, including most of the harmful substances found in tobacco smoke. Smoking one marijuana cigarette deposits about four times more tar into the lungs than a filtered tobacco cigarette.

- Harvard University researchers report that the risk of a heart attack is five times higher than usual in the hour after smoking marijuana.

is that there's a belief in society that there's nothing wrong with alcohol or marijuana. I've never talked to anyone who stopped with alcohol or marijuana. They always go on to something else."[5]

The federal government explains in a fact sheet on marijuana that the illegal drug has negative consequences. The Office of National Drug Control Policy writes:

- Smoking marijuana also weakens the immune system and raises the risk of lung infections. A Columbia University study found that a control group smoking a single marijuana cigarette every other day for a year had a white-blood-cell count that was 39 percent lower than normal, thus damaging the immune system and making the user far more susceptible to infection and sickness.

- Users can become dependent on marijuana to the point they must seek treatment to stop abusing it. In 1999, more than 200,000 Americans entered substance abuse treatment primarily for marijuana abuse and dependence.

- More teens are in treatment for marijuana use than for any other drug or for alcohol. Adolescent admissions to substance abuse facilities for marijuana grew from 43 percent of all adolescent admissions in 1994 to 60 percent in 1999.

- Marijuana is much stronger now than it was decades ago. According to data from the Potency Monitoring Project at the University of Mississippi, the tetrahydrocannabinol (THC) content of commercial-grade marijuana rose from an average of 3.71 percent in 1985 to an average of 5.57 percent in 1998. The average THC content of U.S. produced sinsemilla (type of cannabis plant) increased from 3.2 percent in 1977 to 12.8 percent in 1997.

Source: U.S. Drug Enforcement Administration, "Exposing the Myth of Smoked Medical Marijuana." http://www.justice.gov/dea/ongoing/marijuana.html.

Although marijuana is sometimes characterized as a "harmless herb," the cultivation, trafficking, and use of the drug have a negative impact on many aspects of our lives, from public health to national security, transportation, the environment, and educational attainment.[6]

Marijuana has many negative health effects. It leads to impairment of the cognitive mind as well as to respiratory problems, and it reduces problem solving. Those who smoke marijuana regularly have increased chances for depression, anxiety, suicidal thoughts, and even schizophrenia.[7] It causes many to have hallucinations, delusions, and paranoid thoughts. It certainly causes individuals to lose some level of cognitive brain functioning and to not be able to operate machinery.

The medical benefits of marijuana are minimal.

Supporters of the marijuana legalization movement tout the drug as an important one for medical purposes. They say that many sick people, such as those with AIDS, glaucoma, and many other ailments, can benefit from the illegal drug medically. The evidence for this claim, however, is at best questionable and debatable. In April 2006, the Food and Drug Administration declared that "no sound scientific studies" exist to confirm that marijuana has positive medicinal purposes.[8] An FDA official declared that "smoked marijuana has no currently accepted or proven medical use in the United States and is not an approved medical treatment."[9] DEA agent Robert Bonner offered a similar assessment in the 1990s: "The data supporting medical use [of marijuana] are almost entirely anecdotal. By any modern standard, marijuana is no medicine."[10]

The U.S. Supreme Court has upheld federal laws against marijuana usage.

In *Gonzalez v. Reich*, the U.S. Supreme Court ruled that the federal government could criminally prosecute even the medicinal use of marijuana. The case arose after law enforcement officials destroyed the marijuana plants of Angel Reich and Diane Monson, two women who used marijuana for medical purposes. They claimed that a California state law, the Compassionate Use Act of 1996, known formally as Proposition 215, supported their right for the medicinal usage of the drug. The federal government, however, countered that the federal Controlled Substances Act trumped any state or local law. In other words, state laws could not supersede federal criminal laws. Of the use of medical marijuana and illegal drugs in general, John P. Walters, the U.S. government's drug czar in 2006, stated:

> We have a responsibility as a civilized society to ensure that the medicine Americans receive from their doctors is effective, safe, and free from the pro-drug politics that are being promoted in America under the guise of medicine.[11]

The public does not want legalization.
The majority of the public does not favor the legalization of marijuana. When polled, most voters use common sense and do

QUOTABLE

John Ray

It is no surprise that a few well-educated, well-to-do folks want to legalize drugs. For them, legalization is the quick, cheap escape from society's nightmare of drug-related crime. It's the wrong way to go. It would be a death sentence for the poor.... I will not sacrifice the poor for an immoral and impractical quick fix. There's a better way to take the crime and violence out of the drug trade. First, let's commit our enormous human and monetary resources to raising a generation of drug-free children.

Source: John Ray, "Legalize Drugs?" *Washington Post*, January 2, 1990, p. 12.

not desire the decriminalization of illegal drugs. Nor does this attitude exist in America alone. In November 1998, for example, voters in Switzerland rejected a proposal that would have turned the country into a free-drug area. Nearly 74 percent of the public rejected the proposal, surprising many experts. The government touted the public's vote as evidence for its crime-fighting initiatives.[12]

Even more significantly, here in the United States in November 2010, voters in California rejected an initiative that would have made it the first state to legalize marijuana beyond medical purposes. The public rejected Proposition 19, also known as the Regulate, Control and Tax Cannibus Act, by a vote of 56 percent to 44 percent. The initiative would have allowed Californians to possess up to an ounce of marijuana and to grow small amounts of marijuana in their homes.

Part of the reason for the public's opposition is that legalizing the recreational use of marijuana tells children and teenagers that it is all right to smoke marijuana. That would be a tragic message to send the nation's youth. As professor Gregory E. Roth wrote:

> Fortunately, most citizens can comprehend this problem. Most citizens know the laws of the United States are based on morals. Most citizens know that marijuana is a dangerous drug to society. And most citizens know it would be wrong for them to support a drug culture more than they support the police actually enforcing the law.[13]

Summary

While some people believe that marijuana use has positive medical effects for some patients suffering from serious illnesses, many others simply want to legalize marijuana for recreational drug-use purposes; they just want to "get high." Legalization should not happen because marijuana is a harmful drug that causes its users all sorts of physical, emotional, and psychological problems. It causes some users to suffer hallucinations. It causes others to become extremely paranoid. It certainly makes all users to become less able to operate a motor vehicle or even to carry on an intelligent conversation.

The Future of the War on Drugs

The war on drugs has been the de facto American policy for decades, regardless of which major political party—Democrats or Republicans—controls Congress or the White House. Illegal drug use in the United States has consumed untold amounts of money, sent an enormous number of people to prison, and led to the deaths of many people, both from violent drug wars and addiction. Despite this, the federal government has continued to fund the war on drugs, believing it needs to be fought wherever necessary to keep drugs out of the hands of American citizens. "The battle is being waged on foreign soil, on the coast and along the Mexican border and on the streets," reporters with the *Los Angeles Times* wrote. "In each, there are problems."[1]

Many critics argue that the war is an abject failure. "The war on drugs has been a disaster for America," Judge Andrew

Napolitano writes.[2] The government has spent millions upon millions of dollars, and yet illegal drugs stream into the country and are made available on city streets. Once on the streets, drugs help to perpetuate an atmosphere of violence and addiction. As a result, many people remain hopelessly trapped in a treacherous life cycle of drug addiction and crime.

Other observers suggest that the war on drugs has had many positive effects. By keeping drugs illegal, fewer people have easy access to them and are therefore less likely to become addicted. Fewer drug addicts means a healthier and more productive society, since it is rare that a drug user can reach his or her full potential as a citizen while being addicted.

In the end, many questions remain about American drug policy. Will more drug courts be established to help those who are hopelessly addicted to drugs? Will more states approve of the medical use of marijuana? Will marijuana ever be legalized like alcohol and tobacco? Will Congress lower even further the ratio between crack and powder cocaine offenses? Will Congress apply the new crack-cocaine sentencing law retroactively to help those who remain locked behind bars for years for trafficking in relatively small amounts of drugs? Will the federal government institute a new policy that will somehow slow down the transport of illegal drugs in this country?

Under the administration of President Barack Obama, there has been an emphasis on treating addiction rather than prosecuting the war on drugs. In May 2009, Gil Kerlikowske, the director of the National Drug Control Policy Office, testified that "the Obama administration understands addiction is a disease, and its treatment needs to be addressed as part of a comprehensive strategy to stop drug use."[3] In an earlier interview, Kerlikowske distanced the administration from the very concept of a war on drugs. "Regardless of how you try to explain to people it's a 'war on drugs' or a 'war on a product,' people see a war as a war on them," he said. "We're not at war with people in this country."[4]

That said, the administration believes that there still needs to be an active national, state, and local law enforcement presence, as Kerlikowske identified later in the year when he testified about the growing dangers of the Mexican drug cartels.

QUOTABLE

Drug Policy Alliance on the War on Drugs

Everyone has a stake in ending the war on drugs. Whether you're a parent concerned about protecting children from drug-related harm, a social justice advocate worried about racially disproportionate incarceration rates, an environmentalist seeking to protect the Amazon rainforest, or a fiscally conservative taxpayer, you have a stake in ending the drug war. U.S. federal, state, and local governments have spent hundreds of billions of dollars trying to make America "drug-free." Yet heroin, cocaine, methamphetamine, and other illicit drugs are cheaper, purer, and easier to get than ever before. . . . The war on drugs has become a war on families, a war on public health and a war on our constitutional rights.

Many of the problems the drug war purports to resolve are in fact caused by the drug war itself. So-called "drug-related" crime is a direct result of drug prohibition's distortion of immutable laws of supply and demand. Public health problems like HIV and hepatitis C are all exacerbated by zero tolerance laws that restrict access to clean needles. The drug war is not the promoter of family values that some would have us believe. Children of inmates are at risk of educational failure, joblessness, addiction, and delinquency. Drug abuse is bad, but the drug war is worse.

Few public policies have compromised public health and undermined our fundamental civil liberties for so long and to such a degree as the war on drugs. The United States is now the world's largest jailer, imprisoning nearly half a million people for drug offenses alone. That's more people than Western Europe, with a bigger population, incarcerates for all offenses. Roughly 1.5 million people are arrested each year for drug law violations—40% of them just for marijuana possession. People suffering from cancer, AIDS, and other debilitating illnesses are regularly denied access to their medicine or even arrested and prosecuted for using medical marijuana. We can do better.

Source: Drug Policy Alliance. http://www.drugpolicy.org/drugwar/.

Decline in teen pot use stalls

The use of marijuana has leveled off after nearly a decade of steady decline.

Marijuana use, in the 12 months prior to the survey

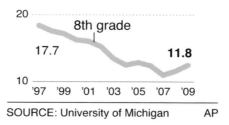

40 percent

38.5

12th grade

32.8

30

20

8th grade

17.7

11.8

10

'97 '99 '01 '03 '05 '07 '09

SOURCE: University of Michigan   AP

This graphic shows marijuana use by U.S. eighth and twelfth graders between 1997 and 2009. During that period, teenage marijuana use decreased, but has leveled off recently.

"The tentacles of international drug trafficking organizations are everywhere, in every community," he testified before a congressional committee, adding:

They operate in our cities, suburbs, rural areas, in our national parks and our public lands, and in our prisons. Without the help of state, local, and tribal law enforcement throughout our country, we will never have the detailed knowledge of local drug trafficking cells and their drug, money, and weapons distribution networks that is necessary to dismantle the international drug trafficking organizations that threaten not only our nation, but also our neighbors throughout the region.[5]

One disturbing phenomenon has been the recent national rise in illegal drug use, particular among young people. There has been a significant increase in the amount of marijuana usage among young people. In the late 1990s, illegal drug use had dropped. That changed in 2009. The federal government believes that "a possible correlation with this phenomenon is that fewer young people today see 'great risk' in using marijuana regularly" as contrasted with young people a decade earlier.[6]

Clearly, there are many unanswered questions surrounding the drug war and the proper courses of action for the country to take. It will be up to policymakers, carefully attuned to the will of the American people, to decide how best to deal with the illegal drug trade in the years ahead.

Beginning Legal Research

The goals of each book in the POINT/COUNTERPOINT series are not only to give the reader a basic introduction to a controversial issue affecting society, but also to encourage the reader to explore the issue more fully. This Appendix is meant to serve as a guide to the reader in researching the current state of the law as well as exploring some of the public policy arguments as to why existing laws should be changed or new laws are needed.

Although some sources of law can be found primarily in law libraries, legal research has become much faster and more accessible with the advent of the Internet. This Appendix discusses some of the best starting points for free access to laws and court decisions, but surfing the Web will uncover endless additional sources of information. Before you can research the law, however, you must have a basic understanding of the American legal system.

The most important source of law in the United States is the Constitution. Originally enacted in 1787, the Constitution outlines the structure of our federal government, as well as setting limits on the types of laws that the federal government and state governments can enact. Through the centuries, a number of amendments have added to or changed the Constitution, most notably the first 10 amendments, which collectively are known as the "Bill of Rights" and which guarantee important civil liberties.

Reading the plain text of the Constitution provides little information. For example, the Constitution prohibits "unreasonable searches and seizures" by the police. To understand concepts in the Constitution, it is necessary to look to the decisions of the U.S. Supreme Court, which has the ultimate authority in interpreting the meaning of the Constitution. For example, the U.S. Supreme Court's 2001 decision in *Kyllo v. United States* held that scanning the outside of a person's house using a heat sensor to determine whether the person is growing marijuana is an unreasonable search—if it is done without first getting a search warrant from a judge. Each state also has its own constitution and a supreme court that is the ultimate authority on its meaning.

Also important are the written laws, or "statutes," passed by the U.S. Congress and the individual state legislatures. As with constitutional provisions, the U.S. Supreme Court and the state supreme courts are the ultimate authorities in interpreting the meaning of federal and state laws, respectively. However, the U.S. Supreme Court might find that a state law violates the U.S. Constitution, and a state supreme court might find that a state law violates either the state or U.S. Constitution.

Not every controversy reaches either the U.S. Supreme Court or the state supreme courts, however. Therefore, the decisions of other courts are also important. Trial courts hear evidence from both sides and make a decision, while appeals courts review the decisions made by trial courts. Sometimes rulings from appeals courts are appealed further to the U.S. Supreme Court or the state supreme courts.

Lawyers and courts refer to statutes and court decisions through a formal system of citations. Use of these citations reveals which court made the decision or which legislature passed the statute, and allows one to quickly locate the statute or court case online or in a law library. For example, the Supreme Court case *Brown v. Board of Education* has the legal citation 347 U.S. 483 (1954). At a law library, this 1954 decision can be found on page 483 of volume 347 of the U.S. Reports, which are the official collection of the Supreme Court's decisions. On the following page, you will find samples of all the major kinds of legal citation.

Finding sources of legal information on the Internet is relatively simple thanks to "portal" sites such as findlaw.com and lexisone.com, which allow the user to access a variety of constitutions, statutes, court opinions, law review articles, news articles, and other useful sources of information. For example, findlaw.com offers access to all Supreme Court decisions since 1893. Other useful sources of information include gpo.gov, which contains a complete copy of the U.S. Code, and thomas.loc.gov, which offers access to bills pending before Congress, as well as recently passed laws. Of course, the Internet changes every second of every day, so it is best to do some independent searching.

Of course, many people still do their research at law libraries, some of which are open to the public. For example, some state governments and universities offer the public access to their law collections. Law librarians can be of great assistance, as even experienced attorneys need help with legal research from time to time.

Common Citation Forms

Source of Law	Sample Citation	Notes
U.S. Supreme Court	*Employment Division v. Smith*, 485 U.S. 660 (1988)	The U.S. Reports is the official record of Supreme Court decisions. There is also an unofficial Supreme Court ("S. Ct.") reporter.
U.S. Court of Appeals	*United States v. Lambert*, 695 F.2d 536 (11th Cir.1983)	Appellate cases appear in the Federal Reporter, designated by "F." The 11th Circuit has jurisdiction in Alabama, Florida, and Georgia.
U.S. District Court	*Carillon Importers, Ltd. v. Frank Pesce Group, Inc.*, 913 F.Supp. 1559 (S.D.Fla.1996)	Federal trial-level decisions are reported in the Federal Supplement ("F. Supp."). Some states have multiple federal districts; this case originated in the Southern District of Florida.
U.S. Code	Thomas Jefferson Commemoration Commission Act, 36 U.S.C., §149 (2002)	Sometimes the popular names of legislation—names with which the public may be familiar—are included with the U.S. Code citation.
State Supreme Court	*Sterling v. Cupp*, 290 Ore. 611, 614, 625 P.2d 123, 126 (1981)	The Oregon Supreme Court decision is reported in both the state's reporter and the Pacific regional reporter.
State Statute	Pennsylvania Abortion Control Act of 1982, 18 Pa. Cons. Stat. 3203-3220 (1990)	States use many different citation formats for their statutes.

Cases

United States v. Clary, 34 F.3d 709 (8th Cir. 1994)

In this decision, a federal appeals court ruled that the crack-cocaine sentencing laws—which had the oft-criticized 100-to-1 ratio for crack to powder cocaine sentences—did not violate the Equal Protection Clause of the Fourteenth Amendment. The appeals court overturned a decision by a federal district court judge who had ruled that the law did violate the Equal Protection Clause.

Gonzales v. Raich, 545 U.S. 1 (2005)

In this decision, the U.S. Supreme Court ruled that federal criminal drug laws trumped state laws that favored medicinal use of marijuana. The Court ruled that the federal government did have the power to regulate medicinal use of marijuana in a single state because it had an impact on interstate commerce.

Kimbrough v. United States, 552 U.S. 85 (2007)

In this decision, the U.S. Supreme Court ruled that federal district court judges—the trial court judges in the federal system—have the ability to impose sentences that are outside the range of the federal sentencing guidelines for crack-cocaine offenses.

Statues

Marihuana Tax Act (50 Stat. 551, Public Law 75-238)

The first federal law dealing with marijuana, it was strictly speaking a tax measure, but its effect was to make the drug all but illegal in this country.

Controlled Substances Act

The Controlled Substances Act is Title II of Comprehensive Drug Abuse Prevention and Control Act of 1970 (Public Law 91-513), and is codified as 21 U.S.C. §§801 and following. The CSA's most important feature is a classification system under which drugs are assigned to "schedules" with varying levels of regulation. Marijuana was placed in Schedule I, meaning that it has a high potential for abuse and no recognized medical use. The CSA also sets out federal penalties for possessing or trafficking in illegal drugs. Marijuana and other drugs are also regulated at the state level, typically by laws modeled after the CSA. In many states, the penalties for possessing or using small amounts of marijuana are less severe than under federal law. More than a dozen states explicitly rule out jail as a punishment for first offenders caught with small amounts.

Proposition 215

In 1996, California voters approved Proposition 215 (codified as California Health & Safety Code §11362.5), which allows qualified patients to possess and use marijuana on a doctor's recommendation. As of 2010, 14 states have enacted some form of medical-marijuana law. These laws do not override the federal CSA, and both doctors and patients can be prosecuted under federal law.

Fair Sentencing Act of 2010

This law (Public Law 111-220) reduced the penalty disparity between crack cocaine and powder cocaine that had been created by the Anti-Drug Abuse Act

of 1986. The federal penalties inequality was reduced from a 100-to-1 ratio to an 18-to-1 ratio as a result of this law, which also removed the mandatory five-year minimum sentencing provision for simple possession of crack.

Terms and Concepts

Addiction
Controlled substance
Crack cocaine
Drug courts
Equal protection
Gateway drug
Recidivism
Sentencing guidelines

Introduction: An Overview of the War on Drugs

1 Judge Andrew P. Napolitano, *Lies the Government Told You: Myth, Power, and Deception in American History.* Nashville, Tenn.: Thomas Nelson Publishers, 2010, pp. 191–192.

2 "Sellers of Weed Must Pay New Tax," *Atlanta Constitution,* September 26, 1937, p. 4K.

3 "The Marijuana Menace," *Washington Post,* April 17, 1937, p. 6.

4 Attorney General Clarence Beck of Kansas, "The Marijuana Menace," *Washington Post,* January 13, 1938, p. X1.

5 Associated Press, "Marijuana Film Barred," *New York Times,* March 26, 1938, p. 5.

6 Martin Arnold, "Narcotics a Growing Problem of Affluent Youth," *New York Times,* January 4, 1965, p. 1.

7 Ibid.

8 Michael Isikoff, "Users of Crack Cocaine Link Violence to Drug's Influence," *Washington Post,* March 24, 1989, p. A11.

9 Jules Witcover, "$5 Billion War Against Drugs in Schools Urged," *Los Angeles Times,* January 31, 1973, p. 4.

10 Steven B. Duke, "Mass Imprisonment, Crime Rates, and the Drug War: A Penological and Humanitarian Disgrace," 9 *Connecticut Public Interest Law Journal* 17, 24 (2010).

11 Jennifer Broxmeyer, "Prisoners of Their Own War: Can Policymakers Look Beyond the 'War on Drugs' to Drug Treatment Courts?" 118 *Yale Law Journal* Pocket Part 17, 17 (2008).

12 Duke, pp. 27–28.

Point: Drug Courts Reduce Crime, Cut Costs, and Save Lives

1 Ruben Rosario, "For 100th Grad: Drug Court Saved His Life," *St. Paul Pioneer Press,* May 19, 2010.

2 Todd Leskanic, "Treatment Court Turns Offenders' Lives Around," *Tampa Tribune,* May 14, 2009, p. 1.

3 Quoted in Sarah Reinecke, "Grad: Drug Court 'Saved My Life,'" *Omaha World-Herald,* June 24, 2010. http://

www.omaha.com/article/20100624/NEWS97/706249813/1015.

4 L.L. Brasier, "Oakland County: Drug Court Programs Help Residents Turn Lives Around," *Detroit Free Press,* March 13, 2009, p. 5.

5 Kristi Jourdan, "New Program Gives Young Drug Addicts a Chance to Restore Their Lives," *Las Vegas Review-Journal,* September 19, 2010, p. 11B.

6 Ronald Smothers, "Miami Tries Treatment, Not Jail, in Drug Cases," *New York Times,* February 19, 1993, p. A10.

7 Quoted in Lisa Arthur, "Judge Won Praise for How He Ran First Drug Court," *Miami Herald,* May 18, 2004, p. 4B.

8 Quoted in Patrick May, "Judge Puts Heart into Drug Court, 61-Year-Old Jurist Is Tough, Tender," *Miami Herald,* October 21, 1990, p. B2.

9 Ibid.

10 Ibid.

11 Mireya Navarro, "Experimental Courts Are Using New Strategies to Blunt the Lure of Drugs," *New York Times,* October 17, 1996, p. A25.

12 C. West Huddleston III, Douglas B. Marlowe, and Rachel Casebolt, "Painting the Current Picture: A National Report Card on Drug Courts and Other Problem-Solving Court Programs in the United States," National Drug Court Institute, May 2008, p. 2. http://www.ndci.org/sites/default/files/ndci/PCPII1_web%5B1%5D.pdf.

13 Michael W. Finigan, Shannon M. Carey, and Anton Cox, "The Impact of a Mature Drug Court Over 10 Years of Operation: Recidivism and Costs," April 2007, p. II. http://www.ncjrs.gov/pdffiles1/nij/grants/219225.pdf.

14 Ibid.

15 Ibid.

16 Interview with Judge Don Ash, November 9, 2010.

17 Quoted in Dina Fine Maron, "Courting Drug-Policy Reform: A Bipartisan Drug Policy 20 Years in the Making?" *Newsweek,* October 7, 2009. http://www.newsweek.com/2009/10/06/courting-drug-policy-reform.print.html.

18 Remarks of Laurie Robinson, assistant U.S. attorney general, Office of Justice Programs, September 30, 2010. http://www.ojp.usdoj.gov/newsroom/speeches/2010/10_0930lrobinson.htm.

19 Interview with Judge Don Ash.

20 Editorial, "Drug Court Works," *Daily Gazette* (Sterling, Ill.), July 24, 2010.

21 Testimony of John K. Roman, Domestic Policy Subcommittee, Oversight and Government Reform Committee, U.S. House of Representatives, July 22, 2010, pp. 2–3. http://www.urban.org/uploadedpdf/901371-drug-courts-pre-trial-diversion.pdf.

22 Jessica Huseman, "Do Drug Courts Work?" National Center for Policy Analysis, August 5, 2010, p. 2. http://www.ncpa.org/pdfs/ba717.pdf.

23 Huddleston, et al., pp. 21–24.

24 Ibid, p. 2.

Counterpoint: Drug Courts Do Not Work and Create Problems

1 Morris Hoffman, "The Drug Court Scandal," 78 *North Carolina Law Review* 1437, 1465 (2000).

2 Don Van Natta Jr. and Jeff Leen, "Is the Program Working? Who Knows?" *Miami Herald*, August 29, 1994, p. A6.

3 Morris Hoffman, "The Rehabilitative Ideal and the Drug Court Reality," 14 *Federal Sentencing Reporter* 172 (2001), citing Barbara E. Smith et al., "Strategies for Courts to Cope with the Caseload Pressures of Drug Cases (ABA, 1991).

4 Hoffman, "The Rehabilitative Ideal."

5 Ryan S. King and Jill Pasquarella, "Drug Courts: A Review of the Evidence," April 2009. http://www.sentencingproject.org/doc/dp_drugcourts.pdf.

6 National Association of Criminal Defense Lawyers, "America's Problem-Solving Courts: The Criminal Costs of Treatment and the Case for Reform," September 2009, p. 11.

7 Ibid., p. 18.

8 Stanton Peele, "Drug Courts: You'd Think They Would Work," *Huffington Post*, June 22, 2010. http://www.huffingtonpost.com/stanton-peele/drug-courts-you-would-thi_b_619681.html.

9 Quoted in National Association of Criminal Defense Lawyers report, p. 23.

10 Ibid.

11 Ibid., p. 12.

12 Ibid., p. 24.

13 "Who Needs Drug Courts?" *Philadelphia Inquirer*, October 17, 2009, p. A10.

14 Michael M. O'Hear, "Rethinking Drug Courts: Restorative Justice as a Response to Racial Injustice," 20 *Stanford Law & Policy Review* 101, 117–120.

15 Ibid., p. 118.

16 Ibid., p. 136.

17 Morris Hoffman, "Drug Courts Don't Work," *USA Today*, October 21, 2008, p. 11A.

18 Ibid.

19 King and Pasquarella, p. 19.

20 Ibid., p. 16.

21 Ibid.

22 Ibid., p. 15.

23 Ibid.

24 O'Hear, "Rethinking Drug Courts," p. 103.

25 Hoffman, "The Drug Court Scandal," p. 1477.

Point: The Sentencing Disparity Between Crack and Powder Cocaine Should Be Eliminated

1 Families Against Mandatory Minimums, "Profiles of Injustice: Stephanie Nodd." http://www.famm.org/ProfilesofInjustice/FederalProfiles/StephanieNodd.aspx.

2 Families Against Mandatory Minimums, "Profiles of Injustice: DeJarion Echols." http://www.famm.org/ProfilesofInjustice/FederalProfiles/DeJarionEchols.aspx.

3 Alyssa L. Beaver, "Getting a Fix on Cocaine Sentencing Policy: Reforming the Sentencing Scheme of the Anti-Drug Abuse Act of 1986," 78 *Fordham Law Review* 2531, 2533–34 (2010).

4 Ibid., 2534.

5 Ibid., 2546.

6 John V. Elmore, *Fighting for Your Life: The African-American Criminal Justice Survival Guide.* Phoenix, Ariz.: Amber Books, 2004, p. 121.

7 Ibid., p. 122.

8 Quoted in Michael York, "Drug Gang Leader Gets Life, Admonishes Court," *Washington Post*, May 15, 1993, p. B1.

9 Quoted in Charisse Jones, "Crack and Punishment: Is Race the Issue?" *New York Times*, October 28, 1995, p. 1.

10 Statement of Lanny A. Breuer, assistant U.S. attorney general, Criminal Division, U.S. Department of Justice, before the U.S. Senate Judiciary Committee, hearing entitled "Restoring Fairness to Federal Sentencing: Addressing the Crack-Powder Disparity," April 29, 2009. http://judiciary.senate.gov/pdf/09-04-29BreuerTestimony.pdf.

11 *United States v. Clary*, 846 F.Supp. 768, 770 (E.D. Mo. 1994).

12 Ibid., 797.

13 United States Sentencing Commission: "Report to Congress: Cocaine and Federal Sentencing Policy" (2002), p. 96.

14 Timothy Egan, "War on Crack Retreats, Still Taking Prisoners," *New York Times*, February 28, 1999, p. 1.

15 Paul Butler, *Let's Get Free: A Hip-Hop Theory of Justice*. New York: The New Press, 2009.

16 Michael O'Hear, "Drug Laws: Policy and Reform: Rethinking Drug Courts: Restorative Justice as a Response to Racial Injustice," 20 *Stanford Law & Policy Review* 463, 475–476 (2009).

17 Quoted in Felisa Cardona, "Federal Sentencing Guidelines Change Today for Some Drug Crimes," *Denver Post*, November 1, 2010. http://www.denverpost.com/news/ci_16487678#ixzz142pjGyOt.

Counterpoint: Crack Cocaine Offenses Should Be Punished at a Higher Rate

1 *United States v. Kimbrough*, 552 U.S. 85, 94 (2007).

2 Randall Kennedy, *Race, Crime, and the Law*. New York: Random House, 1997, p. 374.

3 Quoted in Charisse Jones, "Crack and Punishment: Is Race the Issue?"

4 Wayne J. Roques, "The Laws Against Crack Protect Society," *New York Times*, June 15, 1994, p. A24.

5 *United States v. Kimbrough*.

6 *United States v. Clary*, 34 F.3d 709 (8th Cir. 1994).

7 Michael Isikoff, "Users of Crack Cocaine Link Violence to Drug's Influence," *Washington Post*, March 24, 1989, p. A11.

8 Ibid.

9 Quoted in David Shribman and Joe Davidson, "Divided Capital: Many in Washington Now Find Drug War Isn't a Distant Affair," *Wall Street Journal*, April 14, 1989, p. A1.

10 Quoted in Charisse Jones, "Crack and Punishment: Is Race the Issue?"

11 Testimony of R. Alexander Acosta, "U.S. Sentencing Commission — Public Hearing on Cocaine Sentencing Policy," November 14, 2006, p. 12. http://www.ussc.gov/Legislative_and_Public_Affairs/Public_Hearings_and_Meetings/20061115/testimony.pdf.

12 Kennedy, *Race, Crime, and the Law*, pp. 370–371.

13 Quoted in Neil A. Lewis, "Justice Department Opposes Lower Jail Terms for Crack," *New York Times*, March 20, 2002, p. A24.

14 Philip Coltoff, "In the War on Drugs, No Honorable Surrender Is Possible," *New York Times*, February 9, 1996, p. A28.

15 Quoted in "War on Crack Retreats, Still Taking Prisoners."

Point: Marijuana Should Be Legalized

1 Sheryl Gay Stolberg, "Government Study of Marijuana Sees Medical Benefits, *New York Times*, March 18, 1999, p. A1.

2 Andy Birkey, "Medical Marijuana Bill Advances in Senate with Moving Testimony," *Minnesota Independent*, February 12, 2009. http://minnesotaindependent.com/26340/medical-marijuana-bill-advances-in-senate-with-moving-testimony.

3 Ibid.

4 Quoted in Editorial, "U.S. Should Put an End to War on Drugs, Legalize Pot," *Denver Post*, April 21, 2009, p. B-10.

5 "Legalize Sale of Marijuana, Magazine Asks," *Los Angeles Times*, November 11, 1963, p. C3.

6 Quoted in Bernard Gavzer, "Should Marijuana Be Legal?" *Washington Post*, June 12, 1994, p. M1.

7 Stolberg, "Government Study of Marijuana Sees Medical Benefits," p. A1.

8 Paul Armentano, "Emerging Clinical Applications for Cannabis and Cannabinoids: A Review of the Recent Scientific Literature, 2000–2010," NORML (January 27, 2010). http://norml.org/pdf_files/NORML_Clinical_Applications_for_Cannabis_and_Cannabinoids.pdf.

9 Michael Neibauer, "D.C. Council Legalizes Medicinal Marijuana," *Washington Business Journal*, May 4, 2010.

10 H.R. 2385 (111th Congress) (introduced June 11, 2009)

11 "Risk of Marijuana's 'Gateway Effect' Overblown, New UNH Research Shows," September 2, 2010. http://www.eurekalert.org/pub_releases/2010-09/uonh-rom083110.php.

12 Ibid.

Counterpoint: Marijuana Is a Harmful, Illegal, and Addictive Drug

1 Quoted in Bernard Gavzer, "Should Marijuana Be Legal?"

2 Ibid.

3 Jim McDonough, "Wrong Lesson from Marijuana Gateway Study," *The Record*, December 17, 2002.

4 Lt. Alfred Sexton quoted in Melissa M. Scallan, "Gateway Drugs Lead to a Treacherous Path," *Sun Herald* (Biloxi, Miss.), October 20, 2003, p. A9.

5 Quoted in Scallan.

6 Office of National Drug Control Policy Fact Sheet, "Marijuana: Know the Facts." http://www.whitehousedrugpolicy.gov/publications/pdf/Marijuana.pdf.

7 Office of National Drug Control Policy Fact Sheet, "Marijuana Legalization: A Bad Idea." http://www.whitehousedrugpolicy.gov/publications/pdf/mj_legal.pdf.

8 Gardiner Harris, "F.D.A. Dismisses Medical Benefit from Marijuana," *New York Times*, April 21, 2006, p. A1.

9 Ibid.

10 Quoted in Gavzer, "Should Marijuana Be Legal?"

11 Quoted in Linda Greenhouse, "Justices Say U.S. May Prohibit the Use of Medical Marijuana," *New York Times*, June 7, 2005, p. A1.

12 Elizabeth Olson, "Swiss Voters Reject Legalization of Heroin, Cocaine and Marijuana," *New York Times*, November 30, 1998, p. A4.

13 Gregory E. Roth, "Marijuana Is a Big Problem," *Des Moines Register*, May 27, 2010, p. A5.

Conclusion: The Future of the War on Drugs

1 Bill Farr and Carol McGraw, "War on Cocaine Fought on 3 Frustrating Fronts," *Los Angeles Times*, September 22, 1986, p. 2.

2 Napolitano, *Lies the Government Told You*, p. 200.

3 Testimony of Gil Kerlikowske, to Domestic Policy Subcommittee, Oversight and Government Reform Committee, May 19, 2009. http://www.whitehousedrugpolicy.gov/news/testimony09/051909_dpc_subcommittee.pdf.

4 Quoted in Gary Fields, "White House Czar Calls for End to 'War on Drugs,'" *Wall Street Journal*, May 14, 2009. http://online.wsj.com/article/SB124225891527617397.html.

5 Testimony of Gil Kerlikowske, "The Rise of the Mexican Drug Cartels and U.S. National Security," Oversight and Government Reform Committee, July 9, 2009. http://www.whitehousedrugpolicy.gov/news/testimony09/070909_ogr_committee.pdf.

6 "Marijuana: Know the Facts," p. 3. http://www.whitehousedrugpolicy.gov/publications/pdf/Marijuana.pdf.

RESOURCES ||||▷

Books and Articles

Allenbaugh, Mark, and Paul Hofer. "The U.S. Sentencing Commission Considers Shortening Terms for Imprisoned Crack Offenders: Should the Reduction of the Disparity Between Crack and Powder Cocaine Sentencing Be Retroactive?" Findlaw Writ, November 19, 2007. Available online. URL: http://writ.news.findlaw.com/commentary/20071119_hofer.html.

Armentano, Paul. "Emerging Clinical Applications for Cannabis and Cannabinoids: A Review of the Recent Scientific Literature, 2000–2010." NORML (January 27, 2010). Available online. URL: http://norml.org/pdf_files/NORML_Clinical_Applications_for_Cannabis_and_Cannabinoids.pdf.

Baum, Dan. *Smoke and Mirrors: The War on Drugs and the Politics of Failure*. New York: Little, Brown and Company, 1996.

Beale, Sara Sun. "The News Media's Influence on Criminal Justice Policy: How Market-Driven News Promotes Punitiveness." 48 *William and Mary Law Review* 397 (2006).

Beaver, Alyssa L. "Getting a Fix on Cocaine Sentencing Policy: Reforming the Sentencing Scheme of the Anti-Drug Abuse Act of 1986." 78 *Fordham Law Review* 2531 (2010).

Belenko, Steven. "Research on Drug Courts: A Critical Review." 1 *National Drug Court Institute Review* 31 (1998).

Berney, Arthur. "Cocaine Prohibition: Drug-Induced Madness in the Western Hemisphere." 15 *Boston College Third World Law Journal* 19 (1995).

Bowers, Josh. "Contraindicated Drug Courts." 55 *UCLA Law Review* 783 (2008).

Broxmeyer, Jennifer. "Prisoners of Their Own War: Can Policymakers Look Beyond the 'War on Drugs' to Drug Treatment Courts?" 118 *Yale Law Journal* Pocket Park 17 (2008).

Casey, Timothy. "When Good Intentions Are Not Enough: Problem-Solving Courts and the Impending Crisis of Legitimacy." 57 *Southern Methodist University Law Review* 4 (2004).

Cutler, Lauren M. "Arizona's Drug Sentencing Statute: Is Rehabilitation a Better Approach to the 'War on Drugs?'" 35 *New England Journal on Criminal and Civil Confinement* 397 (2009).

Dionne, Lee. "Let the Punishment Fit the Crime: Should Courts Exercise the Power of Appellate Sentence Review in Cases Involving Narcotics and Other Stigmatized Crimes?" 99 *Journal of Criminal Law and Criminology* 255 (2009).

Duke, Steven B. "Drug Prohibition: An Unnatural Disaster." 27 *Connecticut Law Review* 571 (1995).

———. "Mass Imprisonment, Crime Rates, and the Drug War: A Penological and Humanitarian Disgrace." 9 *Connecticut Public Interest Law Journal* 17 (2010).

Elmore, John V. *Fighting for Your Life: The African-American Criminal Justice Survival Guide.* Phoenix, Ariz.: Amber Books, 2004.

Finigan, Michael W., Shannon M. Carey, and Anton Cox. "The Impact of a Mature Drug Court Over 10 Years of Operation: Recidivism and Costs." April 2007. Available online. URL: http://www.ncjrs.gov/pdffiles1/nij/grants/219225.pdf.

Gray, James P. *Why Our Drug Laws Have Failed and What We Can Do About It: A Judicial Indictment of the War on Drugs.* Philadelphia, Pa.: Temple University Press, 2001.

Hoffman, Morris. "The Drug Court Scandal." 78 *North Carolina Law Review* 1437 (2000).

———. "The Rehabilitative Ideal and the Drug Court Reality." 14 *Federal Sentencing Reporter* 172 (2001).

Huddleston, C. West III, Douglas B. Marlowe, and Rachel Casebolt. "Painting the Current Picture: A National Report Card on Drug Courts and Other Problem-Solving Court Programs in the United States." National Drug Court Institute, May 2008. Available online. URL: http://www.ndci.org/sites/default/files/ndci/PCPII1_web%5B1%5D.pdf.

Huseman, Jessica. "Do Drug Courts Work?" National Center for Policy Analysis, August 5, 2010. Available online. URL: http://www.ncpa.org/pdfs/ba717.pdf.

Kennedy, Randall. *Race, Crime and the Law.* New York: Random House, 1997.

King, Ryan S., and Jill Pasquarella. "Drug Courts: A Review of the Evidence," April 2009. Available online. URL: http://www.sentencingproject.org/doc/dp_drugcourts.pdf.

Miller, Eric J. "Embracing Addiction: Drug Courts and the False Promise of Judicial Interventionism." 65 *Ohio State Law Journal* 1479 (2004).

National Association of Criminal Defense Lawyers. "America's Problem-Solving Courts: The Criminal Costs of Treatment and the Case for Reform." September 2009. Available online. URL: http://www.nacdl.org/public.nsf/2cdd02b415ea3a64852566d6000daa79/665b5fa31f96bc40852574260057a81f/$FILE/problem-solvingreport_110409_629(K+PMS3145).pdf.

O'Hear, Michael. "Rethinking Drug Courts: Restorative Justice As a Response to Racial Injustice." 20 *Stanford Law & Policy Review* 101 (2009).

Sklansky, David A. "Cocaine, Race and Equal Protection." 47 *Stanford Law Review* 1283 (1995).

Steer, John R., with Mark H. Allenbaugh. "The State of Federal Cocaine Sentencing Policy: Will Congress Soon Finish What the U.S. Sentencing Commission Started?" Findlaw Writ, February 18, 2008. Available online. URL: http://writ.findlaw.com/allenbaugh/20080218.html.

Tison, Elizabeth. "Amending the Sentencing Guidelines for Cocaine Offenses: The 100-to-1 Ratio Is Not As 'Cracked' Up As Some Suggest," 27 *Southern Illinois University Law Journal* 413 (2003).

United States Sentencing Commission. "Report to the Congress: Cocaine and Federal Sentencing Policy" (2002). Available online. URL: http://www.ussc.gov/Legislative_and_Public_Affairs/Congressional_Testimony_and_Reports/Drug_Topics/200205_RtC_Cocaine_Sentencing_Policy/200205_Cocaine_and_Federal_Sentencing_Policy.pdf.

————. "Report to the Congress: Cocaine and Federal Sentencing Policy" (2007). Available online. URL: http://www.ussc.gov/Legislative_and_Public_Affairs/Congressional_Testimony_and_Reports/Drug_Topics/200705_RtC_Cocaine_Sentencing_Policy.pdf.

Vagins, Deborah J., and Jesselyn McCurdy. "Cracks in the System: Twenty Years of the Unjust Federal Crack Cocaine Law" (2006). Available

online. URL: http://www.aclu.org/pdfs/drugpolicy/cracksinsystem_20061025.pdf.

Web Sites

American Civil Liberties Union

http://www.aclu.org

This broad-based civil liberties group advocates against the war on drugs and for the legalization of marijuana and has consistently opposed the strong penalties against crack-cocaine offenses compared with powder-cocaine offenses.

Drug Policy Alliance

http://www.drugpolicy.org/

This is, in its own words, "the nation's leading organization promoting alternativves to the drug war."

DrugSense

http://www.drugsense.org/

This nonprofit group seeks to inform the public about drug-policy reform efforts.

Families Against Mandatory Minimums

http://www.famm.org/

This organization's Web site declares that it is "the national voice for fair and proportionate sentencing laws. We shine a light on the human face of sentencing, advocate for state and federal sentencing reform, and mobilize thousands of individuals and families whose lives are adversely affected by unjust sentences."

National Association of Criminal Defense Lawyers

http://www.nacdl.org

This group of criminal defense lawyers advocates on a broad array of issues dealing with criminal justice. It has some resources that are balanced on the question of drug courts.

National Drug Court Institute

http://www.ndci.org

This organization's Web site has a plethora of information about drug courts, including detailed studies and overviews of how the courts have performed.

National Organization for the Reform of Marijuana Laws

http://norml.org/

This organization advocates for the legalization of marijuana and for the medicinal uses of marijuana.

Office of National Drug Control Policy

http://www.whitehousedrugpolicy.gov

This is the federal government's chief agency dealing with the nation's drug laws and drug policies.

Partnership for a Drug-Free America

http://www.drugfree.org

This nonprofit organization seeks to help parents prevent drug use by their children or help find interveention or treatment programs for children already addicted to drugs.

Stop the Drug War

http://www.stopthedrugwar.org

This organization opposes the consistent governmental policies that are described as furthering the "war on drugs."

DAVID L. HUDSON JR. is a First Amendment Scholar at the First Amendment Center at Vanderbilt University. He teaches law classes at Middle Tennessee State University, Nashville School of Law, and Vanderbilt Law School. He is the author or coauthor of more than 20 books, including several in the POINT/COUNTERPOINT series.

ALAN MARZILLI, M.A., J.D., lives in Birmingham, Ala., and is a program associate with Advocates for Human Potential, Inc., a research and consulting firm based in Sudbury, Mass., and Albany, N.Y. He primarily works on developing training and educational materials for agencies of the federal government on topics such as housing, mental health policy, employment, and transportation. He has spoken on mental health issues in 30 states, the District of Columbia, and Puerto Rico; his work has included training mental health administrators, nonprofit management and staff, and people with mental illnesses and their families on a wide variety of topics, including effective advocacy, community-based mental health services, and housing. He has written several handbooks and training curricula that are used nationally and as far away as the territory of Guam. He managed statewide and national mental health advocacy programs and worked for several public interest lobbying organizations while studying law at Georgetown University. He has written more than a dozen books, including numerous titles in the POINT/COUNTERPOINT series.